WOODEN

WOODEN

A LIFETIME OF OBSERVATIONS AND REFLECTIONS ON AND OFF THE COURT

COACH JOHN WOODEN
with STEVE JAMISON

New York   Chicago   San Francisco   Lisbon   London   Madrid   Mexico City
Milan   New Delhi   San Juan   Seoul   Singapore   Sydney   Toronto

Library of Congress Cataloging-in-Publication Data

Wooden, John R.
    Wooden: a lifetime of observations and reflections on and off the court /
John Wooden and Steve Jamison.
        p.   cm.
    ISBN 0-8092-3041-0
    1. Wooden, John R.   2. Basketball coaches—United States—Biography.
3. Coaching (Athletics)—Philosophy.   4. Conduct of life.   I. Jamison, Steve.
II. Title.
GV884.W66A38   1997
796.323'092—dc21   97-00564
[B]   CIP

Excerpt on page 8 is reprinted with the permission of Scribner, a Division of Simon & Schuster, from *The Poems of Henry Van Dyke* (New York: Scribner, 1920).

Every effort has been made to determine and acknowledge copyrights, but in some cases copyright could not be traced. The publisher offers apologies for any such omission and will rectify this in subsequent editions upon notification.

37 38 39 40 41 42   QFR/QFR   1 5 4 3

ISBN 978-0-8092-3041-9
MHID   0-8092-3041-0

Cover illustration by Dan Krovalin

McGraw-Hill books are available at special quantity discounts to use as premiums and sales promotions or for use in corporate training programs. To contact a representative, please visit the Contact Us pages at www.mhprofessional.com.

Reflections on Coach Wooden

JOHN WOODEN is a "philosopher-coach" in the truest sense: a man whose beliefs, teachings, and wisdom go far beyond sports, and ultimately address how to bring out the very best in yourself and others in all areas of life.

He is a master teacher who understands motivation, organization, and psychology. Coach Wooden is able to successfully share his wisdom because he has a gift for expressing his philosophy directly and simply, in a manner accessible and applicable to everyone.

Coach Wooden's own life is the embodiment of enduring American values. His priorities are, and always have been, correct—family, faith, and friends—and he never veered from them in spite of professional success and celebrity of the highest magnitude.

John Wooden is an American legend who would be as comfortable among the ancient sages as he is welcomed and respected by today's citizens and leaders. He is a very special American.

Bill Walsh
Former Head Football Coach
San Francisco 49ers

John Wooden *is* the greatest basketball coach of all time, but what I learned from him had much more to do with living life than with playing ball.

The skills he taught us on the court—teamwork, personal excellence, discipline, dedication, focus, organization, and leadership—are the same tools that you need in the real world. Coach showed us how these skills are transferable. He wasn't just teaching us about basketball, he was teaching us about life.

John Wooden taught us how to focus on one primary objective: Be the best you can be in *whatever* endeavor you undertake. Don't worry about the score. Don't worry about image. Don't worry about the opponent. It sounds easy, but it's actually very difficult. Coach Wooden showed us how to accomplish it.

Coach gained respect with a very simple method: by his personal example. He worked harder, longer, smarter, and was more dedicated, loyal, concerned, caring, detailed, meticulous, and enthusiastic than anyone I have ever worked with.

John Wooden never had to tell you that he was the one in charge or get up and give rah-rah speeches to get your attention. He led by being himself.

You saw how true he was to doing things right, by *thinking* right. Coach Wooden was more interested in the process than in the result. This was very important to him. He really wanted things done correctly and it started with the way he did things. You wanted to follow him and his example.

For us, it all started with our practices at UCLA, which were nonstop action and absolutely electric, super-charged, on edge, crisp, and incredibly demanding, with Coach Wooden pacing up and down the sidelines like a caged tiger, barking out instructions, positive reinforcement, and appropriate maxims: "Be quick, but don't hurry." "Failing to prepare is preparing to fail." "Never mistake activity for achievement." "Discipline yourself and others won't need to."

At the same time he constantly moved us into and out of minutely detailed drills, scrimmages, and patterns while exhorting us to "Move . . . quickly . . . hurry up!" It was wonderfully exhilarating and absolutely intense.

In fact, games actually seemed like they happened in a slower gear because of the pace at which we practiced. We'd run a play perfectly in scrimmage and Coach would say, "OK, fine. Now re-set. Do it again, faster." We'd do it again. Faster. And again. Faster. And again.

I'd often think during UCLA games, "Why is this taking so long?" because we had done everything that happened during a game thousands of times at a faster pace in practice.

Coach Wooden wasn't one to casually throw around compliments. He expected you to be really good. Being really good wasn't something special. He assumed you'd be on top of things because that's the way he was. He didn't think you needed to be complimented for doing what was normal.

However, as players we knew we were rising to a greater level when we'd see that smile on his face. When four guys touched the ball in two seconds and the fifth guy hit a lay-up, man, what a feeling! When things really clicked, the joy of playing was reflected by the joy on his face. He created an environment where you expected to be your best and outscore the opponent; where capturing a championship and going undefeated was part of the normal course of events. Coach made the extraordinary seem normal.

I can't describe how exciting it was to be a part of that—the joy he created in preparing us for competition. Of course, the real competition he was preparing us for was life (even though I didn't realize that until much later). His lessons were invaluable to me when I started raising a family and pursuing other professional activities beyond basketball.

After my father, Coach Wooden has had the most profound influence on me of anyone in my entire life. I was touched by Coach Wooden's greatness—he set a standard I have been trying to live up to ever since. He is as positive as you get. He taught us the values and characteristics that could make us not only good players, but also good people. He taught us how to be true to ourselves while also striving to be our best.

Now I'm forty-four years old and I'm telling my four teenage sons what Coach Wooden used to tell his players. I'm even writing his maxims on their lunch bags and then listening to them complain about it, just like I used to complain.

They'll see. My kids will learn. Soon enough they'll come to understand and appreciate the great wisdom of a very wise man: Coach John Wooden.

I have nothing but the greatest love and respect for Coach. Thanks for your sacrifice, gifts, and patience.

Bill Walton
College Basketball Hall of Fame
NBA Hall of Fame

COACH WOODEN was first of all a teacher. I believe he takes more pleasure from teaching than from all the recognition he amassed during his illustrious career.

As an assistant coach under Coach Wooden, I learned more about organizing your time, planning, evaluating, and teaching than in all my years of college put together. He was a master at organizing what needed to be done down to the last detail and then teaching it the same way.

I believe his longevity at the top of the college basketball ladder was no accident. His willingness to listen to the ideas of others and his lack of ego allowed him to change and keep up with the ever-changing game. But don't let that fool you into thinking he was soft. He was as tough a competitor as I have ever met at everything we ever did together. From cribbage to snooker to free-throw shooting, he gave no quarter and asked none in return. He wanted to beat you at your best—and usually did.

His life away from basketball has been dominated by his family and church. Other than his writing and reading, his spare time is spent caring for and loving his family and God. I have never met a nicer or more dedicated family man than Coach Wooden.

It is very difficult to put into words what Coach has meant to me both personally and professionally. I guess it would suffice to say that along with my father, he has had a tremendous influence on my life. To try to emulate him both on and off the floor is very difficult to do. He is such a wonderful person in every way. I can't imagine what my life would have been had Coach Wooden not been my guiding light. As the years pass, I appreciate him more and more and can only pray that I can have half as much influence on the young people I coach as he has had on me.

May God bless my coach, John Wooden.

Denny Crum
Head Basketball Coach
University of Louisville

FROM THE DAY I met Coach Wooden, I had the utmost confidence in him. It didn't take me very long to appreciate the "coolness" he possessed. Coach taught us self-discipline, and was always his own best example. He discouraged expressing emotion on the court, stressing that it would eventually leave us vulnerable to opponents.

To this day I can see my coach, calm and confident, twisting a game program between his hands, showing that he shared the players' excitement.

The wisdom of Coach Wooden had a profound influence on me as an athlete, but an even greater influence on me as a human being. He is responsible, in part, for the person I am today. Coach and I were simpatico from the beginning—that has always meant a great deal to me, both on and off the court.

> *Kareem Abdul-Jabbar*
> *College Basketball Hall of Fame*
> *NBA Hall of Fame*

A MAN OF John Wooden's accomplishments and integrity would stand out in any era, but now, more than two decades after he coached his last game, he is in some ways an even more striking figure. He remains the rare sports giant without a marketing plan, without something to hype or sell.

As a coach he was able to adapt to changing circumstances without bending to every trend, without compromising what was at his core. His understanding always went beyond the moment; his thoughts and actions guided by enduring principles no less valid today than seventy years ago back home in Martinsville, Indiana. Perhaps that is why, even now, he retains a compelling voice that never has to be raised to be heard.

Bob Costas
NBC Sports

IN THE COURSE of a lifetime, almost everyone is positively affected by someone in a life-changing way. Such a person and I crossed paths twenty-six years ago. His love and commitment to living life to the fullest have walked with me all my days since then and are continuing to change me day by day.

His name is John Wooden. Such a simple and common name, isn't it? But so was Ben Franklin, Tom Jefferson, and many others. Coach Wooden is a simple man, but a man who understands life like no other I have ever met. In my opinion, he has mastered the art of living by practicing simple wisdom in all situations. In every area of life he has pursued excellence and understanding. Just as a master mechanic knows all the workings of an automobile, Coach Wooden truly understands the workings of life. Someone once said, "The person who knows 'how' will always have a job. The person who knows 'why' will be his boss." John Wooden understands "how" and "why" as they pertain to life and that is why it seems like he is playing chess when everyone else is just playing checkers.

John Wooden is truly a remarkable man. His simple wisdom and love have changed the course of my life, and for that I will always be grateful.

Swen Nater
Representative
Price Costco

For all the wonderful young people with whom I've had the pleasure of working throughout my career.
And, for Nellie. You are with me always.

—COACH JOHN WOODEN

For my dad, Everett, who began a lifetime of leading, teaching, and coaching as conductor of his Hal Leonard Orchestra and who helped bring this book about.
For my mother, Mary; as warm as a summer breeze, pretty as a mile of roses, and funny as an Irish angel.
For John Wooden. Thank you for your trust.

—STEVE JAMISON EDSTROM

Contents

PART IV: PUTTING IT ALL TOGETHER: MY PYRAMID OF SUCCESS   165

Preface

Steve Jamison

An Uncommon Man

Does any sports figure in the twentieth century stand astride the record books with more authenticity and authority than Coach John Wooden, the legendary teacher of basketball at the University of California at Los Angeles? He is the architect of perhaps the greatest championship record in all of sports.

> 1964, 1965, 1967, 1968, 1969,
> 1970, 1971, 1972, 1973, 1975

Each of those years, he produced another National Collegiate Athletic Association (NCAA) championship for the UCLA team he coached—altogether ten of them in twelve years, including seven national championships in a row. In a row!

Think for a moment about how that compares to what came before and what has followed. John Wooden shattered all notions of what constitutes supremacy in college basketball and, some would argue, supremacy in any sport. Quite simply, he went where no one had ever gone before or since.

But there is more: 88 consecutive victories (previous record, 60), 38 straight NCAA tournament wins (previous record, 13), and eight undefeated Pac-8 (Pacific conference) crowns. Undefeated season after undefeated season bringing coach of the year award after coach of the year award, including selection as *Sports Illustrated*'s sportsman of the year in 1972. A lifetime winning percentage of over 80 percent.

But there is more. John Wooden was a three-time All-American while playing basketball at Purdue University and is the only man ever elected to college basketball's hall of fame as *both* player and coach. For many, the magnitude of his achievements in basketball is nearly beyond comprehension.

So let me tell how this book came to be written, because it had little to do with tips on the technique of shooting a jump shot or specific details of Wooden's extraordinary life.

In 1996 I interviewed Coach Wooden in conjunction with a book I was writing called *In the Zone*. When I reviewed the transcripts of what he had said, it became very clear that Coach Wooden's personal philosophy of achievement, success, and excellence has much greater application to living one's life than to playing or coaching basketball. Ultimately what John Wooden addresses is how to achieve peace of mind.

His is a message, and he himself a living example, that goes to the very core of old-fashioned American ideals, principles, and virtues. Much more than basketball titles, championships, or records, this is what Coach John Wooden is all about.

This truth became even more evident as I got to know him. Coach Wooden is pure of heart, modest, trusting, humble, understated, serene, without pretense or hidden agenda, sincere, straightforward, intelligent, quick, confident, and filled with such a profound decency and tremendous inner strength that it is humbling.

Only later did some other qualities also become evident. Coach is ferociously dedicated, meticulously detailed, and as principled as a saint. (This Preface is the only part of the book I have not presented for his review. He would have crossed out most of what I have just written. "Too much," he would say with a gentle smile on his face. "Don't write all of this about me.")

In July I called him and suggested we work on this book idea together. Coach Wooden responded, "I really can't take on another project at this time."

It hadn't occurred to me that this man, now in the middle of his eighth decade, is busy much of the time with personal appearances and seminars around the country, interviews, coaching clinics, and family responsibilities with his seven grandchildren and ten great-grandchildren.

I sent him a letter explaining that the book would be neither a conventional narrative, a biography, nor a how-to book on basketball. It would simply be a presentation in the most direct manner of his philosophy and lessons of life as told in his own special style, a philosophy that started on the little family farm back in Indiana.

It is a philosophy that resulted in a life that has been full and rich in every way and has direct application to each of us.

Most of all, I suggested that *Wooden: A Lifetime of Observations and Reflections On and Off the Court* would allow him yet another opportunity to teach. And I reminded him that first and foremost he considers his profession to be teaching.

While Coach Wooden has never explained to me why he changed his mind about doing this book, I suspect this goes to the heart of it. It allows him another opportunity to do what he loves doing most—namely, teaching life's lessons.

Coach, I'm glad you changed your mind. Your message, your example, and your philosophy are greatly needed in today's America.

Reader, I believe you will share my sentiments as you absorb the words of a very wise, very strong man.

A True North

Our ships are tossed
Across the night,
Our compass cracked,
For wrong or right.
True North is there,
Or over here?
Confusion rules
Our sea is fear.
Then suddenly a beacon bright
Is shining through
This stormy night.
It's pure and straight
To his true course.
The coach is seen.
He is True North.

—Steve Jamison

WOODEN

PART I

FAMILIES, VALUES, VIRTUES

I am just a common man who is true to his beliefs.

—JOHN WOODEN

My Roots Go Deep in America

I was born on a Friday morning in a little place called Hall, Indiana. It was just after the turn of the twentieth century—October 14, 1910.

Dad and Mother raised my three brothers and me on a small farm in the south-central part of the state, until hard times forced our family to move into the nearby town of Martinsville.

What I learned back there during those early years in Indiana—the training I got from my father and mother— has stayed with me all my life. That training started with the kind of people my parents were.

Nothing Is Stronger than Gentleness

My dad, Joshua Wooden, was a strong man in one sense, but a gentle man. While he could lift heavy things men half his age couldn't lift, he would also read poetry to us each night after a day working in the fields raising corn, hay, wheat, tomatoes, and watermelons.

We had a team of mules named Jack and Kate on our farm. Kate would often get stubborn and lie down on me when I was plowing. I couldn't get her up no matter how roughly I treated her. Dad would see my predicament and walk across the field until he was close enough to say "Kate." Then she'd get up and start working again. He never touched her in anger.

It took me a long time to understand that even a stubborn mule responds to gentleness.

My Mother's Great Example

My mother, Roxie Anna, had a hard life living and working and raising a family in our little white farmhouse outside Martinsville. She did the washing, scrubbing, ironing, cooking, mending, and canning with no electricity and no inside plumbing. She did it all herself without any modern conveniences while helping with the farming and bringing up four rambunctious young sons: Maurice, me, Daniel, and William.

At night, during the heat of the Indiana harvest season, Mother would offer us cool slices of watermelon as we sat out on our front porch looking up into the stars.

She gave me my first "basketball," a wobbly thing sewed together using rolled-up rags she had stuffed into some black cotton hose. Dad nailed an old tomato basket with the bottom knocked out to one end of the hayloft in the barn. That's how I got started playing the game of basketball.

Each day my mother demonstrated great patience and the ability and eagerness to work very hard without complaint.

I learned from her what hard work really means and that it's part of life. Hard work comes with the territory. She always knew what had to be done and she did it.

Mother provided a model for how to do my job regardless of the particular circumstances.

The Real Coaches and Teachers

A father and mother must be there to set an example for their children, strong and positive models of what to be and how to behave when the youngsters grow up.

Being a role model is the most powerful form of educating. Youngsters need good models more than they need critics. It is one of a parent's greatest responsibilities and opportunities.

Too often fathers neglect it because they get so caught up in making a living they forget to make a life.

Strong Inside

My father had great inner strength. He was strong in his moral principles, values, and ideals, and like any good father he wanted to instill them in his four sons.

He did that in the manner by which he lived his life.

Life's Game Plan Starts Early

Dad was one of the wisest people I have ever known, in spite of the fact that both he and Mother had only high-school educations. My father created a desire in us to learn to read (including some of the Bible every day). He was a very religious man without being overt about it. Like Mother, he believed in hard work.

He was a good man, strong and positive, who wouldn't speak ill of anyone. Dad was quiet, but when he did say something, he *said* something.

He was the kind of man I set out to be. He was the model.

Two Sets of Threes

My father had what he called his "two sets of threes." They were direct and simple rules aimed at how he felt we should conduct ourselves in life. The first set was about honesty:

Never lie.
Never cheat.
Never steal.

It required no explanation. My brothers and I knew what it meant and that he expected us to abide by it.

The second set of threes was about dealing with adversity:

Don't whine.
Don't complain.
Don't make excuses.

Some people today may think these are naive or kind of corny. But think a moment about what they mean and who you become if you abide by them. That isn't naive. You don't become corny.

Dad's two sets of threes were a compass for me in trying to do the right thing and behaving in a proper manner.

Pride or Punishment

Joshua Wooden was a disciplinarian, but not from a physical point of view. I'd almost rather have taken a whipping than hear him say he was disappointed in something I'd done.

I wanted to please him and not let him down with my behavior. It wasn't a fear of punishment that motivated me. It was my desire to live up to his model and expectations.

Later, as a teacher, I wanted those under my own supervision to be motivated in the same way, to strive to be their best because I believed in them rather than from any fear of punishment.

The Gift of a Lifetime

When I graduated from our little three-room grade school in Centerton, Indiana, I got dressed up in clean overalls for the big event. For my graduation present Dad gave me an old, wrinkled two-dollar bill that he probably had been hanging onto for some time.

He said, "Johnny, as long as you have this you'll never be broke," and he was pretty close to right. Eventually I gave it to my own son Jim.

Dad also gave me something that day that would shape my entire life: my work, my marriage, my goals, my entire philosophy. It was a card on which he had written a few guidelines. I still carry it with me. On one side was this verse by the Reverend Henry Van Dyke:

> Four things a man must learn to do
> If he would make his life more true:
> To think without confusion clearly,
> To love his fellow-man sincerely,
> To act from honest motives purely,
> To trust in God and Heaven securely.

The little verse was straightforward but profound: think clearly, have love in your heart, be honest, and trust in God.

On the other side of the paper, Dad had written out his creed. At the top of the paper, it said "Seven Things to Do." It read as follows:

1. Be true to yourself.
2. Help others.
3. Make each day your masterpiece.
4. Drink deeply from good books, especially the Bible.
5. Make friendship a fine art.
6. Build a shelter against a rainy day.
7. Pray for guidance and count and give thanks for your blessings every day.

All he said when he gave me the little note he had written was, "Son, try and live up to these things."

I wish I could say I have lived up to them. I have tried. Over the years, as I've attempted to follow his creed, I've gained a deeper understanding of it. Let me share what it means to me after all these years.

Be True to Yourself

If we are not true to ourselves, we cannot be true to others—our wife or husband, our family, our profession and colleagues.

As Polonius said to his son Laertes in William Shakespeare's *Hamlet*, "This above all: to thine own self be true, and it must follow, as the night the day, thou canst not then be false to any man."

This is so true, and I believe it is the first point in Dad's creed for a reason. You must know who you are and be true to who you are if you are going to be who you can and should become.

You must have the *courage* to be true to yourself.

Help Others

Oh, the great joy there is in helping others, perhaps the greatest joy! You cannot have a perfect day without helping others with no thought of getting something in return. When we are helping others with the thought of getting something back, it's not the same at all.

Sharing and giving of yourself is joyous. James Russell Lowell wrote:

> It's not what we give but what we share,
> For the gift without the giver is bare.
> Who gives of himself of his alms feeds three,
> Himself, his hungering neighbor, and me.

The basic precept of all the great religions is the Golden Rule: Do unto others as you would have them do unto you. Simply stated, it means, "Help others."

Jesus said, "It is more blessed to give than to receive." We say those words, but how often do we really believe them? They are always true.

You can never acquire happiness without giving of yourself to someone else without the expectation of getting something back.

When it comes to giving, I remind myself what Ralph Waldo Emerson said: "Rings and jewels are not gifts, but apologies for gifts. The only true gift is a portion of thyself."

Make Each Day Your Masterpiece

When I was teaching basketball, I urged my players to try their hardest to improve on that very day, to make that practice a masterpiece.

Too often we get distracted by what is outside our control. You can't do anything about yesterday. The door to the past has been shut and the key thrown away. You can do nothing about tomorrow. It is yet to come. However, tomorrow is in large part determined by what you do today. So make today a masterpiece. You have control over that.

This rule is even more important in life than basketball. You have to apply yourself each day to become a little better. By applying yourself to the task of becoming a little better each and every day over a period of time, you will become a *lot* better. Only then will you be able to approach being the best you can be. It begins by trying to make each day count and knowing you can never make up for a lost day.

If a player appeared to be taking it easy in practice, I told him, "Don't think you can make up for it by working twice as hard tomorrow. If you have it within your power to work twice as hard, why aren't you doing it now?"

If you sincerely try to do your best to make each day a masterpiece, angels can do no better.

Drink Deeply from Good Books, Including the Bible

Poetry, biographies, and all the other great books will greatly enrich your life. There are so many that are so good, and they are all available to you. The poetry Dad read to us when we were kids instilled a love of reading, English, books, and knowledge.

It was a priceless gift and one that has enhanced my own life so much. Drink deeply from those great books of your own choosing and you will enrich yourself.

Make Friendship a Fine Art

Don't take friendship for granted. Friendship is giving and sharing of yourself. If just one side works at it, it isn't friendship. You must work at friendship. Make it a fine art. Go more than halfway. It is two-sided, just like marriage.

Someone is not a good friend because he or she does good things for you all the time. It's friendship when you do good things for each other. It's showing concern and consideration. Friendship is so valuable and so powerful. We take it for granted, but we shouldn't.

> At times when I am feeling low,
> I hear from a friend and then
> My worries start to go away
> And I am on the mend.
>
> In spite of all that doctors know,
> And their studies never end,
> The best cure of all when spirits fall
> Is a kind note from a friend.
>
> —*John Wooden*

The first and most important step in friendship is being a friend.

Build a Shelter Against a Rainy Day

This is not necessarily a material shelter. Your faith, whatever it may be, is the greatest shelter of all. In many ways we've been taken in by materialism. I'm not saying possessions are unimportant, but we often put them out of proportion, ahead of family, faith, and friends.

Pray for Guidance and Count and Give Thanks for Your Blessings Every Day

So often we fail to acknowledge what we have because we're so concerned about what we want. We fail to give real thanks for the many blessings for which we did nothing: our life itself, the flowers, the trees, our family and friends. This moment. All of our blessings we take for granted so much of the time.

A wise person once observed, "How much more pleasant this world would be if we magnified our blessings the way we magnify our disappointments."

And, of course, with that we must also pray for guidance. One of my players at UCLA once told me he was embarrassed to have anyone know that he prayed. There's no shame in praying for guidance. It's a sign of strength.

Living Up to Dad's Creed

I am now in my eighth decade and I would like to be able to tell you that I lived up to Dad's creed, but I am more like the fellow who said:

> I am not what I ought to be,
> Not what I want to be,
> Not what I am going to be,
> But I am thankful that
> I am better than I used to be.

It's important to keep trying to do what you think is right no matter how hard it is or how often you fail. You never stop trying. I'm still trying.

Give It Away to Get It Back

There is a wonderful, almost mystical, law of nature that says three of the things we want most—happiness, freedom, and peace of mind—are always attained when we give them to others.

Six of Life's Puzzlers

- Why is it easier to criticize than to compliment?
- Why is it easier to give others blame than to give them credit?
- Why is it that so many who are quick to make suggestions find it so difficult to make decisions?
- Why can't we realize that it only weakens those we want to help when we do things for them that they should do for themselves?
- Why is it so much easier to allow emotions rather than reason to control our decisions?
- Why does the person with the least to say usually take the longest to say it?

Trusting Others

It has been said that you will be hurt occasionally if you trust too much. This may be true, but you will live in torment if you do not trust enough.

Trusting is part of our higher nature. Doubting is a lower instinct. The latter is easy to do, the former more difficult—but so much more rewarding.

Politeness and Courtesy

You've heard the expression "Politeness and courtesy are a small price to pay for the goodwill of others." In fact, I've used it myself from time to time even though I don't really agree with it.

Being polite and courteous isn't paying a price any more than smiling or being happy is paying a price. You get more than you give when you are polite and courteous. You don't pay. You are paid.

What You Are

A favorite observation of my dad's was the following: "Never believe you're better than anybody else, but remember that you're just as good as everybody else." That's important: No better, but just as good!

I attempted to keep that in mind both when we weren't winning national championships and when we were. It helped me avoid getting carried away with myself.

It goes back to the importance of having strong guidance and role models in the home. That's where the standards are set.

Nellie and I Agreed to Be Agreeable

Nellie Riley caught my eye the first time I ever saw her back at Martinsville High School in Indiana. It was on a warm star-filled night at the carnival during the summer of my freshman year. I think we probably fell in love right away and didn't even know it.

Folks think Nellie and I had a perfect marriage, but it was because we worked at it. There are rough patches in any marriage. Very early we understood that there would be times when we disagreed but there would never be times when we had to be disagreeable. We kept to that rule for over half a century.

Nellie and I have a great love for one another, but we understood that even love takes some work.

Passion Isn't Love

Love is more than passion. Passion is temporary. It isn't lasting. Love, real love, lasts.

Love and Marriage

Love means many things. It means giving. It means sharing. It means forgiving. It means understanding. It means being patient. It means learning. And you must always consider the other side, the other person. You can give without loving, but you cannot love without giving.

And all those things you must not take for granted, but continue to work at.

I agree with Abraham Lincoln. He once said that the best thing a man can do for his children is to love their mother.

Marriage Is Not Courtship

Of course, love is the first characteristic of a good husband or a good wife. If you have the love you should have, you'll find everything else is there if you work at it.

Young couples get married and don't realize it's different from courtship. You have to work at your marriage; it's two-sided, and you'd better realize that.

I had a successful basketball career, but I believe I had an even more successful marriage. In both work and marriage you must be considerate and sincerely care about the welfare of the other person.

When Marriage Weakens

Did your marriage start from love? Of course it did. So, look back. Were you more considerate then? Have you lost that for some reason? Marriage requires that each partner listen to the other side. It's like what I say about leadership: "You must be interested in finding the best way, not in having your own way."

The same is true in marriage. Don't be stubborn and insist on having your own way. Look to find a way that works for both of you.

Team Wooden

People ask if I raised my own family the way I ran the UCLA basketball team. I tell them, "No, I ran the team pretty much like I ran my family." Only with the family I had the greatest co-coach working alongside me, by the name of Nellie.

Family First

This may seem like false modesty, but it isn't intended to be. I am happy my teams at UCLA and elsewhere did well and we earned a measure of recognition. But all of that is nothing compared to my family: Nellie, our two children, our seven grandchildren, and all ten of our great-grand-children. All that love is immeasurable.

My great-granddaughter, Cori, asked me the other day, "Papa, how much longer are you going to live?" I had to chuckle because when you're my age, people tend to be a little more diplomatic with questions like that.

"Cori, dear," I said, "why do you ask me that?"

"Because I will be able to drive a car in six more years and I want you to teach me how, Papa."

I thought, "What an honor she has given me."

Your family is what counts, and you must always remember that as you get caught up in your own professional responsibilities.

I'm very proud of the fact that while all the records were being set at UCLA by our basketball teams, I felt exactly the same way. Family is first. Always. Always.

Sports, Books, and Kids

Most kids, especially boys, are drawn to sports and would rather pick up a basketball or baseball than a book. This is where parents must guide the youngster's thinking.

Sports are fine, but children must be exposed to other things by their mothers and fathers, and that includes books, reading, learning.

My own love of poetry came directly from my dad's willingness to read to all his boys each night back on the farm. I was exposed to reading very early on and developed a love for it before I even realized it. It has stayed with me—to my great benefit—all of my life. All three of my brothers became teachers.

A child must develop a love of academics early, and it usually doesn't just happen. Mom and Dad have to provide the guidance with how they spend their time.

Parents, Children, and Goals

A parent can help direct a child when it comes to goals. Show leadership. Show discipline. Show industriousness. Have traditional values. The person you are is the person your child will become.

Mentors

Mentors, adults who provide direction and a good example, are very important to youngsters. I know this because I had three who were so important in my life.

Mr. Earl Warriner was my country grade-school principal, teacher, and coach back in Centerton, Indiana. From Mr. Warriner I learned that there are no "stars" or privileged individuals.

He would not compromise his principles for the sake of convenience, although he recognized the right of individuals to differ in their opinions on issues. And when he was wrong, he demonstrated that he was man enough to admit it without rationalization or alibi.

My Martinsville high-school coach, Mr. Glenn Curtis, had a tremendous talent for getting individuals and teams to rise to great heights, to near their uppermost level of competency. He was also a fine teacher of fundamentals whom I tried to emulate in my own teaching later on.

And Mr. Ward ("Piggy") Lambert, my coach at Purdue University, demonstrated extraordinary devotion to his principles and was willing to suffer whatever consequences that entailed.

For example, Coach Lambert believed that all intercollegiate games should be played on or near the campus of one of the participating schools. This, of course, ran counter to what was required in the playoffs, where games were often played on distant courts.

Coach felt this deprived the students of the colleges involved and imposed an unfair travel burden on them. He also believed it was inappropriate to hold intercollegiate competitions in commercial venues.

In 1940 Purdue University won the Big Ten title and along with it a trip to the playoffs in Madison Square Garden. Coach Lambert subsequently withdrew Purdue's basketball team from the national tournament. Indiana, the team that had finished just behind Purdue in the standings, was the replacement team and won the national championship that year. Coach Lambert held to his principles. He was true to his beliefs.

My goodness, how fortunate I was as a youngster to have been positively influenced by these adults. I believe that we have an obligation as adults to help youngsters in a similar manner. Mr. Lambert, Mr. Curtis, and Mr. Warriner: great teachers, leaders, coaches.

A Parent Talks to a Child
Before the First Game

This is your first game, my child. I hope you win.
I hope you win for your sake, not mine.
Because winning's nice.
It's a good feeling.
Like the whole world is yours.
But, it passes, this feeling.
And what lasts is what you've learned.

And what you learn about is life.
That's what sports is all about. Life.
The whole thing is played out in an afternoon.
The happiness of life.
The miseries.
The joys.
The heartbreaks.

There's no telling what'll turn up.
There's no telling whether they'll toss you out in
    the first five minutes or whether you'll stay for
    the long haul.

There's no telling how you'll do.
You might be a hero or you might be absolutely
    nothing.
There's just no telling.
Too much depends on chance.
On how the ball bounces.

I'm not talking about the game, my child.
I'm talking about life.
But, it's life that the game is all about.
Just as I said.

Because every game is life.
And life is a game.
A serious game
Dead serious.

But, that's what you do with serious things.
You do your best.
You take what comes.
You take what comes
And you run with it.

Winning is fun.
Sure.
But winning is not the point.

Wanting to win is the point.
Not giving up is the point.
Never being satisfied with what you've done
    is the point.
Never letting up is the point.
Never letting anyone down is the point.

Play to win.
Sure.
But lose like a champion.
Because it's not winning that counts.
What counts is trying.

—Unknown

You Are More Influential than You Think

Like it or not, we have influence of many different kinds in many different places and should conduct ourselves in an appropriate manner. This verse is correct:

More often than we e'er suspect,
The lives of others we do affect.

Superstars who don't want the responsibility that comes with public acclaim don't have that choice. They are role models whether they like it or not; they cannot simply announce that they intend to shirk their responsibility. They are role models, either good or bad.

So are you. So am I. I believe we have an obligation to make that model a positive one.

Commend, Don't Criticize

When a child does something well, commendation is a powerful tool. One of the most powerful motivating tools you can use is the pat on the back. Yes, occasionally the pat must be a little lower and a little harder, but too often parents neglect the praise. They are quick to criticize and slow to commend.

Parenting and Coaching

I think parenting and coaching or teaching are the same thing. And they are the two most important professions in the world.

Parents are coaches, the first coaches a child has. Too many parents expect the coaches and teachers at school to do what they are not doing at home. The parents must set the foundation early. It is often too late by the time a child goes to school.

My Favorite Four-Letter Words: "Kids" and "Love"

The greatest word in the whole dictionary is *love*. Love your children. Listen to them. Share with them. Remember that love is the most powerful medicine in the world.

Do not force them or drive them too hard. Set the example of what you want them to be. Try always to be a good model.

Children are impatient. They want to do right, but maybe they don't know how. Maybe you haven't taught them how. Being a good example is a powerful teaching device. This verse is accurate:

> No written word
>   nor spoken plea
> Can teach our youth
>   what they should be.
>
> Nor all the books
>   on all the shelves.
> It's what the teachers
>   are themselves.
>   —*Unknown*

I think that's it. Those teachers and coaches are the mothers and fathers, and their most powerful tool is love.

Character

Be more concerned with your character than your reputation. Character is what you really are. Reputation is what people say you are. Reputation is often based on character—but not always.

Character is how you react to things—sensibly, without getting carried away by yourself or your circumstances. A person of character is trustworthy and honest, and for a dollar he or she will give you a dollar.

The other kind of person looks for the easy way out.

I like to think the players I coached, however they came to UCLA, left as men of character. But in truth, if they didn't have it when they came, I couldn't give it to them. By then it was too late. That's a job for a mother and father.

The Fundamental Goal

The goal in life is just the same as in basketball: make the effort to do the best you are capable of doing—in marriage, at your job, in the community, for your country. Make the effort to contribute in whatever way you can.

You may do it materially or with time, ideas, or work. Making the effort to contribute is what counts. The *effort* is what counts in everything.

Perfection

Perfection is what you are striving for, but perfection is an impossibility. However, *striving* for perfection is not an impossibility. Do the best you can under the conditions that exist. That is what counts.

Our teams at UCLA had four perfect seasons, but we never played a perfect game, never played as well as we could. That's perfection. We didn't reach perfection, but we constantly strove toward it.

I believe there is nothing wrong with the other fellow being better than you are if you've prepared and are functioning in the way you've tried to prepare. That's all you can do.

But there is something wrong if you've failed to measure up to your ability because you haven't prepared.

Priorities

My parents and early teachers tried to instill these priorities: family, faith, and friends. I've lived my life valuing those things most of all.

Family? Obviously. Friends? Of course. And I tell people I definitely believe in God. I just hope God believes in me.

Learn Forever, Die Tomorrow

Early on I came to believe that you should learn as if you were going to live forever, and live as if you were going to die tomorrow. What does this mean? In the simplest way, I would explain it like this.

Always be learning, acquiring knowledge, and seeking wisdom with a sense that you are immortal and that you will need much knowledge and wisdom for that long journey ahead. Know that when you are through learning, you are through.

But I want to live that life as if I were going to die tomorrow: with relish, immediacy, and the right priorities. I also will not waste even a minute.

Faults Are Fine

I probably have all the same faults anyone has, and so do you. There's nothing wrong with that. Having faults means you're human; you're alive and breathing. There's nothing wrong with having faults so long as you work conscientiously to correct them.

How hard you work at correcting your faults reveals your character.

Timeless Traits

Some say I believe in old-fashioned traits: courtesy, politeness, and consideration. I do believe in these qualities, but they aren't old-fashioned. They never go out of style—even when they seem to be increasingly scarce.

I believe they are still common. We just see their opposites so much in the media that we think that's all there is.

People like to help, to be polite, to be considerate. I believe it's basic human nature. And it's a funny thing: when you start displaying courtesy, politeness, and consideration, people start displaying them right back.

Giving and Receiving

I'm old enough to remember when President Calvin Coolidge observed, "No person was ever honored for what he received. Honor has been the reward for what he gave."

It was true back then and it's still true today.

Are You Looking for the Right Things?

There's an old story about a fellow who went to a small town in Indiana with the thought of possibly moving his family there. "What kind of people live around here?" he asked the attendant at the local filling station.

"Well," the attendant replied as he checked the oil, "what kind of people live back where you're from?"

The visitor took a swallow of his cherry soda and replied, "They're ornery, mean, and dishonest!"

The attendant looked up and answered, "Mister, you'll find them about like that around here, too."

A few weeks later, another gentleman stopped by the gas station on a muggy July afternoon with the same question. "Excuse me," he said as he mopped off his brow. "I'm thinking of moving to your town with my family. What kind of people live around these parts?"

Again the attendant asked, "Well, what kind of people live back where you're from?"

The stranger thought for a moment and replied, "I find them to be kind, decent, and honest folks."

The gas station attendant looked up and said, "Mister, you'll find them about like that around here, too."

It's so true. You often find what you're looking for.

Apples

Every year you hear about a few bad apples in one profession or another: law, religion, business, anything. But the percentage of bad apples is tiny, probably about the same as it's always been. The percentage of good apples is large. We just don't hear about them.

People complain about all the bad politicians and it does seem that so many of them running for office are being dishonest (some perhaps without realizing it). They make promises they know they can't keep and cast harsh aspersions on one another.

Still, it's about the same in that regard as it's always been: plenty of good ones and a few who get all the attention.

The vast majority of Americans are good: the mothers and fathers, the working people, the children, the vast overwhelming majority—millions and millions and millions. A small, small percentage are otherwise. They get the attention.

But we mustn't forget the tremendous good we have within us as a people. I have a very positive opinion of America and our citizens. My opinion of the media and what they try to tell us about ourselves is perhaps not quite as high (although there, too, the majority of them are good and mean well).

The media play up what's wrong more than what's right, and most of what we have is right. As we work to correct what is wrong, we must always keep in mind all the things that are right with America and Americans.

Bringing Out the Best in People

People want to believe you are sincerely interested in them as persons, not just for what they can do for you. You can't fake it. If you don't mean it, they know it—just as you'd know if someone were pretending to be interested in you.

In the workplace you'll get better cooperation and results if you are sincerely interested in people's families and interests, not simply how they do their job. This will bring productive results. Most people try to live up to expectations.

It always comes back to courtesy, politeness, and consideration.

Indiana and Basketball

Way back when I grew up in Indiana in the twenties, people were nuts for basketball, just like they are today. I fell in love with it too, starting with that tomato basket nailed to the hayloft in our barn. Here's a little example of how the people in my hometown felt about the game.

When I went to high school in Martinsville, there was a sign posted outside town that read: Martinsville, Indiana, pop. 4,800. However, our high-school gymnasium seated 5,200 people, 400 more than lived in the whole town! And it was much like that all over the state. Our gym was always full for games.

When the state basketball tournament was played at Butler Field House, the seating was about 18,000, but they could have sold far more tickets for every game. I grew up in that hotbed of basketball where people were absolutely nuts for it.

I didn't think so at the time, but in reflection maybe we had it out of proportion.

Five More Puzzlers

- Why is it so difficult to realize that others are more likely to listen to us if first we listen to them?
- Why is it so much easier to be negative than positive?
- Why is it so difficult to motivate ourselves when we know that results come only through motivation?
- Why is it so difficult to say thank you to someone when those are two of our own favorite words to hear?
- Why do we dread adversity when we know that facing it is the only way to become stronger, smarter, better?

The Family Has Changed

The family unit has suffered since World War II, perhaps because so many men and women left the home to go off to war or to work in factories related to the war effort. They realized after the war that they could have more material things if they continued to work outside the home.

This has increased more and more right up the present day. The result? More and more latchkey children, kids whose parents are both away too much.

I am inclined to feel that our society as a whole has become so infatuated with material things that we have gotten away from the fundamental values and ideals. We seek happiness in the wrong places and in the wrong form.

This is not to say people weren't interested in material things before World War II, but that's when it really seemed to start.

Now parents will say, "We're just trying to make ends meet," and they're telling the truth. But if you think too much about the pursuit of material things, you're going to hurt those youngsters you're working so hard to buy material things for.

The Greatest Joy

Happiness is in many things. It's in love. It's in sharing. But most of all, it's in being at peace with yourself knowing that you are making the effort, the full effort, to do what is right.

True happiness comes from the things that cannot be taken away from you. Making the full effort to do the right thing can never be taken away from you.

I believe the greatest joy one can have is doing something for someone else without any thought of getting something in return.

Peer Pressure

Youngsters today often blame others for their own conduct. I tell youngsters at basketball clinics, "If you're blaming these things on others, doing it simply because they are, that shows weakness on your part. You're making excuses. Giving yourself an alibi, trying to condone what you're doing. You're blaming somebody else, and that's weakness.

"You know what's right and wrong. I know you do."

It's the poorest excuse in the world to say, "Well, somebody else did it, so I have to do it." That's no different from saying, "I've got to rob a bank because the other fellow did."

It goes right back to the first point on Dad's seven-point creed: Be true to yourself. You know what's right. Don't let someone else decide for you.

Accepting Our Responsibility

There have been many wars fought and millions of lives lost because leaders differed with other leaders in regard to religion or race. You and I must accept some accountability for future bloodshed if each and every day we don't do something in our own way to alleviate prejudice in ourselves or others.

A Lesson on Emotion and Language

My older brother, Maurice, and I were cleaning out adjoining stalls in the barn early one Saturday morning when he tossed a pitchfork's worth of manure in my face. I was furious and went after him. He was three years older than me, so I couldn't do much against him at the time. But in the process I called him a name I shouldn't have.

My father overheard it and gave me the only real licking I ever got. I knew I had it coming, so I accepted it a little better than I might have otherwise. Maurice got a good smacking, too. I believe it was even harder than mine.

For whatever reasons, I learned something that has stayed with me to this very day and has been very important to me throughout my life: control your temper and don't use profanity.

Of course, it's a lot easier to avoid the latter if you remember the former.

A Reminder: Be True to Yourself

In 1932, the year I graduated from college, the old professional basketball league out East broke up and a team of players from the original New York Celtics was getting ready to go around the country on a barnstorming tour.

I had been an All-American for three years at Purdue University, as well as College Player of the Year, and because of that had gotten a lot of publicity. The Celtics offered me $5,000 to join them on the tour.

At the time, $5,000 was a huge sum. A job where I would teach five English classes a day and coach four sports in addition to being athletic director would bring in only $1,500 a year.

While playing professional basketball was neither what I had planned to do nor what I had studied in class, I was very tempted to go barnstorming.

I went to my college coach, Piggy Lambert, a man of extremely high principles, and told him about the offer. I asked for his advice on what to do.

Coach Lambert thought for a moment as he shuffled some papers around on his desk. Finally he looked up at me and said, "That's a lot of money, isn't it, John?"

I smiled and chuckled self-consciously. "Yes, it sure is, Coach. It's a lot of money."

Coach Lambert didn't respond immediately. Then he asked, "Is that what you came to Purdue for?"

I was puzzled. "What do you mean, Coach?" I replied.

"I mean, did you come to this university so you could go out traveling around in professional athletics?"

I blinked, cleared my throat, and stared down at my shoes. "No, I didn't come here to do that, sir. I came to get an education."

"Let me ask you something, John. Did you get an education?"

"Yes, I believe I did, sir. A good one," I replied.

"Well," he said, "then maybe you should use it. But that's a decision you'll have to make. I can't decide for you. You'll have to decide for yourself."

Coach Lambert had given me my answer. He had gotten me back to Dad's first creed: Be true to yourself.

Deep down I had known what the correct decision was. Coach Lambert just helped bring it out. I really wanted to teach and coach.

In life, we're not always lucky enough to have someone help us with important decisions. Most of the time you have to figure it out for yourself and it may be confusing and difficult. You'll usually do all right, though, if you have the courage to be true to yourself.

Make Fate Your Friend

Fate plays a part in each of our lives. I was teaching and coaching at Indiana State Teachers College when I was offered coaching positions at both the University of Minnesota and UCLA. I was inclined to go with Minnesota because it was in the Midwest, but there was a little hitch in the offer. They wanted me to keep Dave McMillan, the fellow I would be replacing, as an assistant.

I didn't think that would be for the best, so they offered to consider giving Mr. McMillan another position at the university, one acceptable to him. However, this would take a few days for the board to determine.

They promised they would call me Saturday at 6:00 P.M. with their decision. I told them if they could make the change and it was acceptable to Mr. McMillan, I would come to Minnesota and coach their basketball team.

Meanwhile, UCLA was waiting for a decision. I told them to call me on Saturday night at 7:00. By then I would know what Minnesota had decided. I informed UCLA that if Minnesota made the offer, I would be staying in the Midwest. But fate stepped in and changed things.

On the day the University of Minnesota was supposed to call me, a blizzard hit the Twin Cities and knocked out all phone service in and around Minneapolis. Unaware of the situation, I waited patiently for the call. None came, not at 6:00, not at 6:30. My phone didn't ring at 6:45.

However, right on the button at 7:00 P.M., UCLA called. I assumed Minnesota had decided against offering me the coaching position, so I accepted UCLA's offer.

Almost immediately after I finished talking with UCLA, the call came through from Minneapolis. I was told about the storm. I was also told that the adjustment had been approved and they were offering me the position of head basketball coach at the University of Minnesota, the job that I really wanted.

Had I been able to terminate my agreement with UCLA in an honorable fashion, I would have done so immediately. But I had given my word just a few minutes before.

If fate had not intervened, I would never have gone to UCLA. But my dad's little set of threes served me well: "Don't whine. Don't complain. Don't make excuses."

I resolved to work hard and do the best job I was capable of—even when I discovered upon arriving at UCLA that I wasn't actually working for the university but rather for the associated students. The president of the student body was actually my boss!

I believe that things are directed in some sort of way. I'm not exactly sure how. I also believe that things turn out best for those who make the best of the way things turn out.

Five More Puzzlers

- Why is it so hard for so many to realize that winners are usually the ones who work harder, work longer, and as a result, perform better?
- Why are there so many who want to build up the weak by tearing down the strong?

- Why is it that so many nonattainers are quick to criticize, question, and belittle the attainers?
- Why is it so hard for us to understand that we cannot antagonize and positively influence at the same time?
- Why is it so much easier to complain about the things we do not have than to make the most of and appreciate the things we do have?

Young Folks, Old Folks

Youth is a time of impatience. Young people can't understand why the problems of society can't be solved right *now*. They haven't lived long enough to fully understand human nature, and lack the patience that eventually brings an understanding of the relatively slow nature of change.

On the other hand, older people often become set in their ways, fear change, and accept problems that should be addressed and resolved.

The young must remember that all good and worthwhile things take time (and that is exactly as it should be). Their elders must remember that although not all change is progress, all progress is the result of change (and to resist or fear change is often to get in the way of progress).

The divide between the young and the old could be greatly lessened by more mutual trust and understanding of the other fellow.

Of course, the responsibility to initiate trust falls on those with more maturity. It is important because I believe when we are out of sympathy with the young, our work in this world is over.

Six Ways to Bring Out the Best in People

1. Keep courtesy and consideration for others foremost in your mind, at home and away.
2. Try to have fun without trying to be funny.
3. While you can't control what happens to you, you can control how you react. Make good manners an automatic reaction.
4. Seek individual opportunities to offer a genuine compliment.
5. Remember that sincerity, optimism, and enthusiasm are more welcome than sarcasm, pessimism, and laziness.
6. Laugh with others, never at them.

Losing Nellie: Peace of Mind

When Socrates was in prison facing imminent and unjust death, his jailers, some of the cruelest men in the land, mocked him and asked, "Why do you not prepare your-self for death?"

He looked at the jailers and replied, "I have prepared for death all of my life by the life I lived." Socrates was at peace with himself. My own faith gave me more peace with myself.

The most difficult thing I've ever experienced was losing Nellie thirteen years ago. We were sweethearts for almost sixty years and married for fifty-three years.

Certain things happen, and you must have faith that there is a reason for them. My faith and my family sustained me.

And now, like Socrates, I have no fear of death. When it comes I can be with her again.

I appreciate this poem, "Lucy," by William Wordsworth:

> She dwelt among the untrodden ways
> Beside the springs of Dove.
> A maid of whom there were none to please,
> And very few to love.
>
> A violet by a mossy stone,
> Half hidden from the eye,
> Fair as a star when only one
> Was shining in the sky.
>
> She lived unknown, and few could know
> When Lucy ceased to be.

But she is in her grave,
And, oh, the difference to me.

—*William Wordsworth*

Death is something that holds no fear for me any longer. I'm at peace.

God's Hall of Fame

This crowd on earth
They soon forget
The heroes of the past.
They cheer like mad
Until you fall
And that's how long you last.

But God does not forget
And in his Hall of Fame
By just believing in his Son
Inscribed you'll find your name.

I tell you, friends,
I would not trade
My name however small
Inscribed up there
Beyond the stars
In that celestial hall.

For any famous name on earth
Or glory that they share
I'd rather be an unknown here
And have my name up there.

—*Unknown*

PART II

SUCCESS, ACHIEVEMENT, COMPETITION

Try not to become a man of success but rather try to become a man of value.

—ALBERT EINSTEIN

Mr. Webster's Definition of Success

Mr. Webster defines success as the accumulation of material possessions or the attainment of a position of power, prestige, or perhaps fame. I certainly think those things can be *indicative* of success, but they are not necessarily success in themselves.

I know many eminently successful people who never made a lot of money and never gained any high position or recognition. They simply and quietly raised a family, worked hard, and had a job that allowed them to take care of their family (though not usually in a lavish style). These individuals and their families are a big success by my definition.

Mr. Webster neglects to mention those folks in his book.

Joshua Wooden's Definition of Success

My dad, Joshua, had great influence on my own personal definition of success, and it has little to do with fortune or fame. Although I probably didn't really understand it at the time, one of the things he tried to get across to me was that I should never try to be better than someone else. Then he always added, "But Johnny, never cease trying to be the best *you* can be. That is under your control. The other isn't."

You have little say over how big or how strong or how smart or rich someone else may be. You do have, at least you *should* have, control of yourself and the effort you give toward bringing out your best in whatever you're doing. This effort must be total, and when it is, I believe you have achieved personal success.

The concept that success is mine when I work my hardest to become my best, and that I *alone* determine whether I do so, became central to my life and affected me in a most profound manner.

Try your hardest in all ways and you are a success. Period. Do less than that and you have failed to one degree or another.

I believe this so strongly and I have practiced it as best I could throughout these many years.

Preparation Is the Prize

Cervantes wrote, "The journey is better than the inn." He is right and that is why I derived my greatest satisfaction out of the preparation—the "journey"—day after day, week after week, year after year.

Your journey is the important thing. A score, a trophy, a ribbon is simply the inn.

Thus, there were many, many games that gave me as much pleasure as any of the ten national championship games we won, simply because we prepared fully and played near our highest level of ability.

The so-called importance of a particular game didn't necessarily add to the satisfaction I felt in preparing for the contest. It was the journey I prized above all else.

A Successful Journey Is the Destination

You know where you'd like to go, whether it's to a national championship in basketball or a particular goal in your business or life. You must also realize that this goal will be simply a by-product of all the hard work and good thinking you do along the way—your preparation. The preparation is where success is truly found.

Set your compass in a chosen direction and then focus your attention and efforts completely on the journey of preparation. A successful journey becomes your destination and is where your real accomplishment lies.

For example, let's say Mr. Grigsby owns a company that manufactures shoes. I believe shoes are simply a by-product for his company. Their real product is the teamwork of people within the company, along with the manufacturing plant and other elements of the business that the leader, Mr. Grigsby, has brought together.

How his company's people work as a team is the product. Shoes are a by-product.

Likewise, in my coaching I informed every player who came under my supervision that the outcome of a game was simply a by-product of the effort we made to prepare. They understood our destination was a successful journey—namely, total, complete, and detailed preparation.

Too often we neglect our journey in our eagerness or anxiety about reaching the goal.

If Mr. Grigsby and his team do this they will manufacture poorly made shoes. If we had done this, UCLA would never have won national championships. If you do it in your life or profession, you will find yourself discontent and operating well below your level of competency.

Failures and Mistakes

I had mistakes, plenty, but I had no failures. We may not have won a championship every year. We may have lost games. But we had no failures. You never fail if you know in your heart that you did the best of which you are capable. I did my best. That is all I could do.

Are you going to make mistakes? Of course. But it is not failure if you make the full effort.

I told my players many times, "Failing to prepare is preparing to fail." If you prepare properly, you may be outscored but *you will never lose*. I wanted our players to believe that to their very souls because I know it is the truth. You always win when you make the full effort to do the best of which you're capable.

I also know that only one person on earth knows if you made your best effort: not your coach, not your employer, not your husband or wife, boyfriend or girlfriend, brother or sister. The only person who knows is you. You can fool everyone else.

Blaming Others

You can make mistakes, but you aren't a failure until you start blaming others for those mistakes. When you blame others you are trying to excuse yourself. When you make excuses you can't properly evaluate yourself. Without proper self-evaluation, failure is inevitable.

The Desire to Win

Players fifty years ago wanted to win just as much as players today. Foot soldiers a thousand years ago wanted to win the battle as much as combat troops today. Athletes today have no greater desire to win than athletes at the first Olympic Games. The desire then and now is the same.

The difference is that everybody worries about it more today because of the media and the attention they give to the question of who's winning and who's losing.

Did I win? Did I lose? Those are the wrong questions. The correct question is: Did I make my best effort? That's what matters. The rest of it just gets in the way.

In classical times, the courageous struggle for a noble cause was considered success in itself. Sadly, that ideal has been forgotten. But it is well worth remembering.

The Infection of Success

You become infected with success when you think that your past is going to have an impact on your future. Oh, it might have an effect on the opposition in that your success may affect *their* thinking. Fine, but do not let it affect what you do.

Learn from the past, don't live in the past. The infection of success can lead you to live in the past, to believe that what happened before is *automatically* going to happen again. When that occurs you have been infected by success.

You have control only over the present, right now. Let me prove it to you. I ask you to do this: change the past. Even the smallest, most incidental, least important thing that happened in the past. Go ahead and show that you can change it.

The future? Again I ask you, change right now something in the future. Can you? Of course not. Your control exists now, in the present, right here.

How you respond to past success can be damaging if you let it infect your thinking, if you let it diminish your preparation in the present for the future. Then you've been infected by success.

Underdogs

I have never gone into a game thinking we were going to lose. Never. Even though there have been games where the experts said there was no way we could win. Even if we were big underdogs I always felt anything could happen. Often enough, I was right.

That's also why I never assumed we were going to win.

The Opinion of Others

Do not become too concerned about what others may think of you. Be very concerned about what you think of yourself.

Too often, we care more about a stranger's opinion of us than our own.

Your opinion of yourself begins on the inside with your character. What do you believe in, and are you willing to stand up for it despite what others may think or say?

It's what my dad meant when he said, "Be true to yourself." This comes first, then the opinion of others.

Pressure

The only pressure that amounts to a hill of beans is the pressure *you* put on yourself. If you're trying to live up to expectations put on you by the media, parents, fans, your employer, or whatever else there may be, it's going to affect you adversely because it brings on worry and anxiety. I think that is the tendency of people who choke under pressure. They're thinking about living up to the expectations of everybody else instead of just doing their job the best they can.

Hindsight

You can always look back and see where you might have done something differently, changed this or that. If you can learn something, fine, but never second-guess your-self. It's wasted effort.

If I put a substitution in during a game at UCLA and he immediately makes a mistake, even a stupid mistake, was my decision wrong? Absolutely not.

It just didn't work out. That was the decision I made based on past experience and without emotionalism. I made it with reason, but it just didn't work out. Things don't always work out. It's also true in life.

Does worrying about it, complaining about it, change it? Nope, it just wastes your time. And if you complain about it to other people, you're also wasting their time. Nothing is gained by wasting all of that time.

The Realistic Optimist

I believe one of my strengths is my ability to keep nega-tive thoughts out. I am an optimist. I believe this results from the fact that I set realistic goals—ones that are dif-ficult to achieve, but within reach. You might say I'm a realistic optimist.

Goals should be difficult to achieve because those achieved with little effort are seldom appreciated, give little personal satisfaction, and are often not very worthwhile.

However, if you set goals that are so idealistic there's no possibility of reaching them, you will eventually become discouraged and quit. They become counter-productive. Be a realistic optimist.

Details Create Success

Question: *How can I become an optimist?*
Answer: Proper preparation and attention to details.

I believe in the basics: attention to, and perfection of, tiny details that might commonly be overlooked. They may seem trivial, perhaps even laughable to those who don't understand, but they aren't. They are fundamental to your progress in basketball, business, and life. They are the difference between champions and near champions.

For example, at the first squad meeting each season, held two weeks before our first actual practice, I personally demonstrated how I wanted players to put on their socks each and every time: Carefully roll the socks down over the toes, ball of the foot, arch, and around the heel, then pull the sock up snug so there will be no wrinkles of any kind.

I would then have the players carefully check with their fingers for any folds or creases in the sock, starting at the toes and sliding the hand along the side of and under the foot, smoothing the sock out as the fingers passed over it. I paid special attention to the heel because that is where wrinkles are most likely.

I would watch as the player smoothed the sock under and along the back of the heel. I wanted it done conscientiously, not quickly or casually. I wanted absolutely no folds, wrinkles, or creases of any kind on the sock.

Then we would proceed to the other foot and do the same. I would demonstrate for the players and then have the players demonstrate for me.

This may seem like a nuisance, trivial, but I had a very practical reason for being meticulous about this. Wrinkles, folds, and creases can cause blisters. Blisters interfere with performance during practice and games. Since there was a way to reduce blisters, something the player and I could control, it was our responsibility to do it. Otherwise we would not be doing everything possible to prepare in the best way.

When a player came to UCLA, I didn't ask him what size shoe he wore. We measured his foot. Why? Because when children are growing up, parents buy shoes bigger than their feet, knowing they are growing fast. The youngster might think he's a size 14 when he's actually a size 13.

Shoes that are a little too big let the foot slide around. This can cause a blister, especially if there's also a fold in the player's sock. I wanted the socks to lie smooth and the shoes to fit correctly.

Next I'd instruct the player on how to lace and tie his shoes precisely: Lace snugly, putting some pressure on each eyelet, and then double-tie each shoe so it won't come undone during a practice or a game.

An untied shoe is never good, but it can be particularly troublesome if it happens during performance. It was something under our control that we could prevent, and so we did.

I insisted that hair be short. Did it have anything to do with style? No. Long hair flies around and can interfere with vision. And the perspiration on longer hair may get in eyes or on the hands. I wanted no interference with a player's vision or ball handling.

In addition, practices were often held in the evening, and when players went outside after practice they were susceptible to catching a cold if their hair was wet. Shorter hair is easier to dry. I didn't want to have a player's head cold interfere with his practice.

Players understood my thinking, but that didn't prevent them from testing me, sometimes in a kidding way. "Coach," one of them asked, "how about a mustache? That won't interfere with my ball handling or vision."

Well, of course, the player was correct. I knew a mustache, properly trimmed and of an appropriate length, would be no problem. I also knew human nature, especially as it applied to youngsters. The short, trimmed mustache would be followed by the handlebar mustache or more. I had no desire to become a mustache inspector as part of my daily responsibility. Thus, no mustaches at all.

These seemingly trivial matters, taken together and added to many, many other so-called trivial matters build into something very big: namely, your success.

You will find that success and attention to details, the smallest details, usually go hand in hand, in basketball and elsewhere in your life.

When you see a successful individual, a champion, a "winner," you can be very sure that you are looking at an individual who pays great attention to the perfection of minor details.

Hopes and Dreams

Having a dream is often like hoping for something. It's easy to let our dreams and our hopes get away from reality.

Youngsters are told, "Think big. Anything is possible." I would never go that strong. I want them to think *positively*, but when you think big you often start thinking too big, and I believe that can be very dangerous.

Wanting an unattainable goal will eventually produce a feeling of "What's the use?" That feeling can carry over into other areas. This is bad.

A youngster may dream of being seven feet tall. Hoping for something of that nature is not productive. We should keep our dreams within the realm of possibility—difficult but possible—and make every effort to achieve them.

I have often been asked when I first started dreaming about winning a national championship. Was it at Indiana State Teachers College or after I arrived at UCLA? Perhaps while I was a college player? I never dreamed about winning a national championship. It happened before I even thought it was possible.

What I was dreaming about each year, if you want to call it that, was trying to produce the best basketball team we could be. My thoughts were directed toward preparation, our journey, not the results of the effort (such as winning national championships). That would simply have shifted my attention to the wrong area, hoping for something out of my control. Hoping doesn't make it happen.

Mix idealism with realism and add hard work. This will often bring much more than you could ever hope for.

Paying the Price

People usually know what they should do to get what they want. They just won't do it. They won't pay the price.

Understand there is a price to be paid for achieving anything of significance. You must be willing to pay the price.

The Worthy Opponent

Can there be any great enjoyment or satisfaction in doing what everybody else can do? What joy can be derived in sports from overcoming someone who is not as capable as you are? But there is great joy and satisfaction in competing against an opponent who forces you to dig deep and produce your best.

That is the only way to get real joy out of the competition itself. The worthy opponent brings out the very best in you. This is thrilling.

Follow Your Bliss?

I hear the saying, "Follow your bliss" now and then. It's probably good advice—unless you pick something that's not so good to be your bliss. I think Timothy Leary followed his bliss. You've got to be careful what your bliss is.

Comparisons

We tend to compare ourselves to others. And in what way? We compare ourselves to others who have more things in a material sort of way.

Don't compare yourself with someone else in this manner. You have no control over his or her material things.

A Worthwhile Goal

The goal I believe is important is the goal of making the most of your abilities. That goal is within your reach.

If pursuing material things becomes your only goal, you will fail in so many other ways. Besides, in time all material things go away.

Tall Versus "Tall"

I told my athletes in basketball, "I don't care if you *are* tall, but I do care if you *play* tall." It's just another way of saying that I judged them by the level of effort they gave to the team's journey.

That's the standard of measurement I used. I could also have told them, "Show me what you can do, don't tell me what you can do."

Too often the big talkers are the little doers.

The Main Ingredient of Stardom

No UCLA basketball player's number was retired while I was coach. Later on, certain numbers were retired, such as Kareem Abdul-Jabbar's number (33), and Bill Walton's number (32).

I was against it in both those cases (and any other case) not because Kareem and Bill weren't outstanding players, but because other fellows who played on our team also wore those numbers.

Some of those other players gave me close to everything they had, even though they aren't as famous and perhaps didn't have the natural gifts Kareem and Bill were blessed with.

For example, Willie Naulls wore number 33 while he was a member of our team. He worked hard, he played hard, he was an All-American. Doesn't he have some claim to the number 33?

The jersey and the number on it never belong to just one single player, no matter how great or how big a "star" that particular player is. It goes against the whole concept of what a team is. The team is the star, never an individual player.

Peace of Mind

Without peace of mind, what do you have? Many people go through life unhappy with what they have regardless of how much they have. No matter how much they accumulate, they never achieve peace of mind because they want more. It never ends for them and they are forever unhappy. Usually it's a result of comparing themselves to others, of trying to keep up with the Joneses.

Did I find peace of mind by winning a national championship in basketball in 1964? Then a second, a third, a fourth, and so on? No. I had my peace of mind as a coach long before a national championship was ever won.

Circle What You Are

Take a moment and draw a circle around the following personal characteristics that you possess: confidence, poise, imagination, initiative, tolerance, humility, love, cheerfulness, faith, enthusiasm, courage, honesty, serenity.

I hope you circled them all because all are within each of us. It is simply up to us to bring them out.

The Biggest Change of All

Perhaps you fret and think you can't make a difference in the way things are. Wrong. You can make the biggest difference of all. You can change yourself. And when you do that you become a very powerful and important force— namely, a good role model.

I believe you can do more good by being good than in any other way.

Personal Glory Is Secondary

The recognition I received at UCLA was fine, but mainly I was happy for the teams and the youngsters on those teams. The recognition I received was not all that important. Recognition appeals to the ego, but it is a secondary consideration and is often counterproductive.

Don't get me wrong. I enjoy a little attention as much as the next person, because I recall a time when there was very little.

When I was discharged from the service in January of 1946, I resumed a position teaching English in South Bend, Indiana, where I had been before enlisting in 1942.

While teaching and coaching there, I was invited to be the featured keynote speaker at a ceremony in neighboring Elkhart, Indiana, to honor those deserving special recognition for that particular school year academically, in sports, and otherwise.

Needless to say, I was greatly flattered that they considered me important enough to be the main speaker at this big event. I gave what I considered to be a good and inspirational speech.

In 1971, they remembered my appearance with a brief item in the retrospective section of the *Elkhart Truth*, the local newspaper. The item for "25 Years Ago Today" read as follows:

Elkhart school officials announced today that John R. Wooden, English teacher–coach from South Bend Central High School, will be the principal speaker at their recognition dinner, although they had hoped to get a prominent person.

So, a little recognition for one's effort is nice. It's when you start to let it affect your behavior, and especially your preparation, that you have let it go to your head.

Individual Honors

From an individual standpoint, I am very proud of the medal I received when I graduated from Purdue University as an athlete with an excellent grade point average. That I did, not the team. Me.

I am proud of that and it is one of the reasons I have always stressed education to young people, particularly those who came under my supervision as coach. I know the importance of getting an education. I know that its benefits last a lifetime.

I am also very proud of the fact that I received the Bellamine Medal because no one in the sports world had ever been given it before. And more so because Mother Teresa, a woman for whom I have the greatest respect in the world, had also been a recipient of that medal. For me to receive that same medal, good gracious sakes! I am proud of that.

However, individual recognition, praise, can be a dangerous commodity. It is given for what was done in the past and can take your mind off what you must do to prepare for the future.

It is best not to drink too deeply from a cup full of fame. It can be very intoxicating, and intoxicated people often do foolish things.

Quick to Judge

Why is it that those who are the quickest to judge are often those in possession of the fewest facts?

Overachievers

No one is an overachiever. How can you rise *above* your level of competency? We're all underachievers to different degrees. You may hear someone say that a certain individual "gave 110 percent." How can that be? You can only give what you have, and you have only 100 percent.

I preferred to judge individuals on the basis of how close they came to giving 100 percent, knowing they would never reach perfection, and they would certainly never reach 110 percent of perfection, but perhaps they would operate near their level of competency when their greatest skill was needed.

Eight Suggestions for Succeeding

1. Fear no opponent. *Respect* every opponent.
2. Remember, it's the perfection of the smallest details that make big things happen.
3. Keep in mind that hustle makes up for many a mistake.
4. Be more interested in character than reputation.
5. Be quick, but don't hurry.
6. Understand that the harder you work, the more luck you will have.
7. Know that valid self-analysis is crucial for improvement.
8. Remember that there is no substitute for hard work and careful planning. Failing to prepare is preparing to fail.

Beating Yourself

The very worst thing you can do is to beat yourself. By that I mean not function to your level of competency because you didn't put out your full effort in all ways.

Maybe you stayed out too late last night. Maybe you were too concerned with individual statistics. Maybe you thought you could just "turn it on" without proper preparation. Maybe you did some other things that were counterproductive, like being impatient.

In other words, you beat yourself. The other guy didn't have to beat you. Now you've got something worth being ashamed of.

Winners Make the Most Mistakes

My coach at Purdue, Piggy Lambert, constantly reminded us: "The team that makes the most mistakes will probably win."

That may sound a bit odd, but there is a great deal of truth in it. The *doer* makes mistakes. Coach Lambert taught me that mistakes come from doing, but so does success.

The individual who is mistake-free is also probably sitting around doing nothing. And that's a very big mistake.

Cashing in on Fame

Many, many people advertise products simply because they are paid to do so. I'm not critical of those who are taking money for, say, promoting a particular brand of athletic shoe. That's their business. I just would not feel comfortable telling someone to use something simply because I'm being paid to say it.

It doesn't seem to be an appropriate way to use one's recognition. If I don't feel comfortable doing it then I'm not going to do it, regardless of how much money they want to pay me. And I've been offered considerable sums over the years to do just that.

I may not have their money, but I do have my peace of mind.

Characteristics of a Team Player

We all fit into different niches. Each of us must make the effort to contribute to the best of our ability according to our own individual talents. And then we put all the individual talents together for the highest good of the group.

Thus, I valued a player who cared for others and could lose himself in the group for the good of the group. I believe that quality makes for an outstanding player. It is also why the best players don't always make the best team. I mean by this that a gifted player, or players, who are not *team* players will ultimately hurt the team, whether it revolves around basketball or business.

Understanding that the good of the group comes first is fundamental to being a highly productive member of a *team*.

All-Time Best Starting Five

1. Industriousness
2. Enthusiasm

3. Condition (mental, moral, and physical)
4. Fundamentals
5. Team spirit

A good sixth player on the bench is attention to details.

Why Teams Fail

No matter how great your product, if your sales department doesn't produce, you won't get the results you want. Different departments must all function well for the company to succeed. Different individuals must also function well for the departments to succeed. It takes all doing their best.

I told players at UCLA that we, as a team, are like a powerful car. Maybe a Bill Walton or Kareem Abdul-Jabbar or Michael Jordan is the big engine, but if one wheel is flat, we're going no place. And if we have brand new tires but the lug nuts are missing, the wheels come off. What good is the powerful engine now? It's no good at all.

A lug nut may seem like a little thing, but it's not. There's a role that each and every one of us must play. We may aspire to what we consider to be a larger role, or a more important role, but we cannot achieve that until we show that we are able to fulfill the role we are assigned. It's these little things that make the big things happen.

The big engine is not going to work unless the little things are being done properly.

Remember that Michael Jordan was with the Chicago Bulls for several years before he ever played in a championship game. Was he talented? Of course he was, but that powerful engine called Air Jordan was in a car with some parts that were not functioning properly.

Of course, when I told the players about their roles and the car with the powerful engine, new tires, and tight lug nuts, I also reminded them the car needed a driver behind the wheel or it would just go around in circles or smash into a tree.

I told them the driver was me.

Orange Peels, Pride, and Productivity

I frequently received letters from custodians after we played an away game telling me our basketball team had left the locker room neater and cleaner than anyone who had visited during the year. The towels were put in bins, soap was picked up off the shower floor, and so forth.

The locker rooms were clean when we departed because I asked the players to pick up after themselves. I believe this is just common courtesy. Somebody's going to have to clean it up, and I see no reason why it shouldn't be the person who messed it up. Are managers and custodians the players' servants?

In basketball we often have orange slices or gum at the half. I see no reason why you should throw those orange peels or gum wrappers carelessly on the floor. There are receptacles for that. Again, it's just common courtesy.

As with many of the rules I had, there are other less obvious but equally important reasons for insisting on them. In this case, it goes to the image of the team, both our self-image and the image others have of us.

I think neatness and courtesy make you feel good about yourself. I believe individuals who feel good about themselves are more productive.

For this same reason, I asked players even during practice to keep shirts tucked in and socks pulled up.

I believe this encourages teamwork and team unity. It establishes a spirit of togetherness that helps mold the team into a solo unit. I really believe that. In fact, perhaps I should say I know it. I've seen it work.

Kareem's Selflessness

I wanted each player to be intently interested in developing his own personal abilities as close to perfection as he could (while knowing that perfection is impossible).

Players like Bill Walton and Kareem Abdul-Jabbar may have more to give in some areas thanks to their God-given gifts. My job was to get them to focus those individual abilities on the welfare of the group as a whole.

This was often a formidable challenge for me because the player might have to sacrifice personally for the group as a whole to do better.

I believe, for example, I could have made Kareem the greatest scorer in college history. I could have done that by developing the team around that ability of his. Would we have won three national championships while he was at UCLA? Never. Besides, he wouldn't have wanted that. He was a very unselfish player, the best kind of player, one who put the welfare of the team ahead of his own personal glory.

Kareem took his great ability to score and sublimated it for the greater good of the team. He was willing to do that. But if either he or I had allowed that scoring ability to dominate, we would have cut down on the contributions of others to the detriment of the team. Kareem put the team ahead of himself.

Mr. Charles Barkley is a tremendous athlete, but he may put self before team. He wants to be with a team that can win a championship, but when he gets to that team he seems more interested in how he does individually than how the team does.

Mr. Dennis Rodman seemed to share that attitude until he found direction from Coach Phil Jackson. The result? When Mr. Rodman directed all his energies to the good of the Chicago Bulls, he became part of a great national championship basketball team. Kareem didn't need direction in this area. He was instinctively the best kind of player: a team player.

Miracles

In looking forward, I never expected miracles to happen. Instead I expected the slow, steady progress that comes with industry and patience.

Miracles were welcome, of course. I just felt more comfortable focusing on that over which I had some degree of control.

Miracles were under Someone Else's control.

Nine Promises That Can Bring Happiness

1. Promise yourself that you will talk health, happiness, and prosperity as often as possible.
2. Promise yourself to make all your friends know there is something in them that is special and that you value.
3. Promise to think only of the best, to work only for the best, and to expect only the best in yourself and others.
4. Promise to be just as enthusiastic about the success of others as you are about your own.

5. Promise yourself to be so strong that nothing can disturb your peace of mind.

6. Promise to forget the mistakes of the past and press on to greater achievements in the future.

7. Promise to wear a cheerful appearance at all times and give every person you meet a smile.

8. Promise to give so much time to improving yourself that you have no time to criticize others.

9. Promise to be too large for worry, too noble for anger, too strong for fear, and too happy to permit trouble to press on you.

Losing and Winning

Long before any championships were ever won at UCLA, I came to understand that losing is only temporary and not all-encompassing. You must simply study it, learn from it, and try hard not to lose the same way again. Then you must have the *self-control* to forget about it.

I've also learned that winning games, titles, and championships isn't all it's cracked up to be, and that getting there, the journey, is a lot *more* than it's cracked up to be.

Please understand that I wanted to win every single game I ever played in or coached. Absolutely. I wanted to win. But, I understood that ultimately the winning or losing may not be under my control. What was under my control was how I prepared myself and our team. I judged my success, my "winning," on that. It just made more sense.

I felt if we prepared fully we would do just fine. If we won, great; frosting on the cake. But, at no time did I consider winning to be the cake.

Sage Advice

Many years ago, a friend told me that the best thing a coach can do is to always come close. As soon as you win it all everybody expects it again, and when you don't win it all again you're considered a loser.

If you just come close, everybody gets to say, "Just wait until next year." Hopes stay high, but expectations don't become extreme.

My friend meant it in a kidding way, but there is some truth to his words.

In 1974 we got to the Final Four once again and could have won our eighth national championship in a row. However, we lost to North Carolina State, the eventual champion, in the semifinals 80–77 in a double overtime. Our championship streak was stopped at seven in a row.

Twelve months later, on March 29, 1975, we came back and won the national championship, our tenth overall, by defeating Kentucky 92–85 in the finals. As we stood waiting for the awards ceremony to begin in the San

Diego Sports Arena, a longtime UCLA booster rushed up to my side and grabbed my arm. As he began wildly shaking my hand he shouted in my ear, "We did it! We did it! You let us down last year, Coach, but we got 'em this year!"

A few minutes earlier we had won the national championship, and all he could think to say was that this was an improvement over how we had let him down the previous year when we had *only* gotten to the semis. His comments didn't upset me. They actually amused me a little bit because they reflected what my friend had said about when you win it all.

The more "successful" you are, the higher and higher the expectations become, the more suspicious people are of you, and the more criticism you receive.

It goes back to focusing on the journey rather than the destination. I was just as satisfied with my efforts in the fourteen years before we won a national championship as I was the final twelve years, when we captured ten championships. In fact, and you may have trouble accepting this, I believe we were *more* successful in some years when we didn't win a championship than in some years when we did.

Those on the outside had a higher level of satisfaction when we won championships, but I didn't. I knew that each of the first fourteen years I made the maximum effort to do the best I was capable of. My effort in the "worst" year was exactly the same as in a championship year.

How the media, alumni, or fans viewed the results of that effort was their concern, not mine.

Fame

Here's what I found upon becoming well-known: you're not anything different from what you were before; at least, you shouldn't be.

Fame is just something other people perceive you to be. You're no different. You're still you. It's their illusion. I didn't want it to become my illusion.

On Talent

Many athletes have tremendous God-given gifts, but they don't focus on the development of those gifts. Who are these individuals? You've never heard of them—and you never will. It's true in sports and it's true everywhere in life.

Hard work is the difference. Very hard work.

Unhappiness Today

It is my observation that the primary cause of unhappiness for most people is simply wanting too much: expect-

ing too much materially, chasing the dollar, overempha-
sizing the material things.

When they don't arrive, unhappiness does.

Make the Most of What You've Got

When I came out to UCLA from Indiana State Teachers
College in 1948, I had been led to believe we'd soon have
an adequate place to practice and play our games. However, that did not occur for almost seventeen years.

During that time I conducted UCLA basketball practice in a crowded, poorly lit, and badly ventilated gym on
the third floor of the Men's Gymnasium building. Much
of the time there was wrestling practice at one end, a
trampoline on the side with athletes bouncing up and
down, and gymnastics practice on the other side. The
gym was known as the "B.O. Barn" because of the odor
when it was busy.

In addition to all of this commotion, cheerleaders in
leotards often practiced alongside the court. Of course,
that brought on some additional distractions.

We had no private locker rooms and no private show-
ers. Players climbed three flights of stairs to a gym that
had just two baskets amidst all of the hubbub.

For sixteen years, I helped our managers sweep and
mop the floor every day before practice because of the
dust stirred up from the other activities. These were hardship conditions, not only for the basketball team, but for

the wrestling and gymnastics team members and coaches as well. You could have written a long list of excuses why UCLA shouldn't have been able to develop a good basketball team there.

Nevertheless, the B.O. Barn was where we built teams that won national championships in 1964 and 1965.

You must take what is available and make the very most of it.

Is My Ford Better than Your Cadillac?

Preparing UCLA for a basketball game with Louisville or Arizona or Duke or Michigan, I would tell my players, "We can't control what those other fellows do to get ready. We can only control what we do to get ready. So let's do our very best in that regard and hope that will be good enough, yes, to outscore them. But let's not worry about that. Instead, let's worry about our own preparation."

Let's say I want to build a car—maybe a Ford or a Chevrolet or a Plymouth. I want to build it the best I can possibly build it. Will it be better than a Cadillac or a Mercedes? That's irrelevant.

If I'm building a Ford, I simply want to build the very best Ford I can build. That's *all* I can do: to come close to *my* level of competency, not somebody else's. I have nothing to do with theirs, only mine.

To worry about whether what I'm building is going to be better than what somebody else is building elsewhere is to worry needlessly. I believe that if I'm worried about what's going on outside, it will detract from my preparation inside.

My concern, my focus, my total effort should be on building the very best Ford I can build. I did that in coaching high-school teams and in coaching college teams. My focus was on making that team, that group of individuals, the best they were capable of becoming, whether it was a Ford or a Cadillac.

Some years I understood we were building a Ford. Other years I felt we were building a Cadillac. The effort put forth in all years was the same: total.

And I was just as proud of our well-built Fords as of our well-built Cadillacs.

Recognizing a Champion

You are in the presence of a true competitor when you observe that he or she is indeed getting the most joy out of the most difficult circumstances. The real competitors love a tough situation. That's when they focus better and function better. At moments of maximum pressure, they want the ball.

You begin to see it as time goes by. Not immediately, but gradually you see that real competitors relish the challenge, the bigger the better. The more difficult the game, the more they improve.

True competitors derive their greatest pleasure out of playing against the very best opponents, even though they may be outscored. The difficult challenge provides the rare opportunity to be their best.

Often great competitors don't quite have the physical skills of more gifted players, but they get more out of what they have at moments of great pressure.

Thus, I base my judgment on not just what they had but how they used it. To what extent did they attempt to bring forth their abilities? To what extent did they accomplish that under maximum pressure?

This is how I identified competitors who had greatness within.

Corporate Competitors

The qualities I observe in successful athletes are common among people who enjoy success in business. Both love the battle, the journey, the challenge. Both of them consider the final outcome a by-product.

Both have what it takes to get there and get fired up when the challenge is formidable. They know it presents the potential for greatness and provides the greatest satisfaction.

Being Too Competitive

Competitiveness must be focused exclusively on the process of what you are doing rather than the result of that effort (the so-called winning or losing). Otherwise you may lose self-control and become tight emotionally, mentally, and physically. I think someone who is too competitive as an individual is overly worried about the final score.

Therefore, I never mentioned winning or victory to my players. I never referred to "beating" an opponent.

Instead I constantly urged them to strive for the self-satisfaction that *always* comes from knowing you did the best you could to become the best of which you are capable. That's what I wanted: the total effort. That was the measurement I used, never the final score.

Is Winning the Only Thing?

Mr. Vince Lombardi is supposed to have said, "Winning isn't everything, it's the only thing." Well, if he said that, I disagree. I believe making the total effort is everything. And that's all I ever wanted and all I ever asked from myself or my players.

It's all you should ever ask for or expect. Understand that you won't actually ever become the best of which you are capable. That's perfection. We can't obtain perfection as I understand it. But we can work, and work *hard*, toward obtaining it. If you do that, you will never lose, in sports or in life.

Ego and Arrogance

Everyone has a certain amount of ego, but you must keep that ego under control. Ego is feeling confident and important, knowing you can do the job. But if you get to feeling that you are too important, that you're indispensable, or that you can do the job without real effort and hard work, without the correct preparation, that's arrogance. Arrogance is weakness. That's why I like this poem:

> Sometime when you're feeling important,
> Sometime when your ego's in bloom,
> Sometime when you take it for granted,
> You're the best qualified in the room.
>
> Sometime when you feel that your going
> Would leave an unfillable hole,
> Just follow this simple instruction
> And see how it humbles your soul.
>
> Take a bucket and fill it with water;
> Put your hand in it up to the wrist.
> Pull it out, and the hole that's remaining
> Is the measure of how you'll be missed.

You may splash all you please when you enter;
You can stir up the water galore;
But stop, and you'll find in a minute,
That it looks quite the same as before.

The moral in this quaint example
Is to do just the best that you can.
Be proud of yourself, but remember,
There is no indispensable man!

—*Ogden Nash*

Work Creates Luck

People have expressed amazement over the fact that between 1967 and 1973 UCLA won seven consecutive national championships. This championship streak began shortly after we moved into modern Pauley Pavilion.

More amazing to me is that earlier UCLA won two national championships, in 1964 and 1965, without a home court and under the hardship conditions I have described in the Men's Gymnasium building. To this day I believe that was more difficult than winning seven championships in a row after we moved to Pauley Pavilion.

But because of those first two hard-earned national titles, something unexpected occurred that had a significant impact on the future of our basketball program.

Kareem Abdul-Jabbar (who at that time still went by the name Lewis Alcindor) saw us play in the finals of the national championships and decided to visit our campus before deciding which college to attend.

Because of Kareem's interest, athletic director J. D. Morgan expedited the construction of Pauley Pavilion so that it would be ready if he chose to attend UCLA in the fall of 1965.

With the assurance that he would be practicing and playing in a good facility and the knowledge that UCLA had outstanding academics, Kareem chose to join us.

But without the hard work under extremely difficult conditions at the B.O. Barn that led to the first two national championships, Kareem Abdul-Jabbar would never have seen us play nor thought of coming to our school. And without his interest in joining us, Pauley Pavilion would have taken much longer to complete.

All of this "luck" did not come from out of the blue. Some very hard work under very tough conditions in the preceding years produced this unexpected good fortune.

Have you noticed in your life how often that seems to occur?

B.O. Barn's Unexpected Reward

For my first three years at UCLA, we played our home games in the B.O. Barn itself. Custodians would set up bleachers that seated about 2,100—until the fire department moved in and cut it down to 1,100. This forced us to play our "home" games elsewhere.

So for almost fourteen years, we traveled around playing those games at Santa Monica City College, Venice High School, Long Beach City College, Long Beach Auditorium, Pan Pacific Auditorium, and elsewhere.

Because of our lack of a real home court an unanticipated benefit occurred. Our team became a much stronger road team because we were virtually on the road all of the time.

I have little doubt this was of considerable advantage to us when we played opponents on their home courts. We were used to the disruption of travel and were more comfortable in "foreign" environments. This was particularly advantageous at tournament time.

Adversity often produces the unexpected opportunity. Look for it. Appreciate and utilize it. This is difficult to do if you're feeling sorry for yourself because you're faced with the adversity.

Character Versus "Character"

A true athlete should have character, not be a character. A character tries to attract attention to himself. He is too interested in showing off and trying to get noticed.

Being an individual is different. Bill Walton was an individual, but he was as fine a team player as you'd want. He put the welfare of the team ahead of personal glory.

Some believe that sports build character. I believe that sports reveal character. I see too many players who are characters today. I like a player *with* character, a player like Bill. Or Kareem.

Right from Wrong

Bill Walton came to my office one afternoon at Pauley Pavilion with a serious question for me. His knees had been causing him increasing pain over the last several months, to a point where it was obvious to anyone watching him play that just running the length of the court hurt him badly.

"Coach," he said, "I've heard that smoking marijuana will reduce the pain in my knees. Is it OK with you if I use it?"

I looked up from my desk and replied, "Bill, I haven't heard that it is a pain reliever, but I have heard that it is illegal."

Tricks of the Trade

If you spend too much time learning the tricks of the trade, you may not learn the trade.

There are no shortcuts. If you're working on finding a short cut, the easy way, you're not working hard enough on the fundamentals. You may get away with it for a spell, but there is no substitute for the basics. And the first basic is good, old-fashioned hard work.

Act Quickly (But Don't Hurry)

When you hurry, you tend to make mistakes. On the other hand, if you can't execute quickly, you may be too late to accomplish your task. It's a delicate but crucial balance.

Your Own Standard of Success

Don't measure yourself by what you've accomplished, but rather by what you should have accomplished with your abilities.

This goes right back to my definition of success. Make the effort to do the best of which you are capable. Can anyone possibly do more than that?

Have you ever heard of Conrad Burke or Doug McIntosh? Probably not, but they were as successful as any players I ever coached at UCLA or anywhere else (including those who went on to play professional basketball). These two players came close to fully maximizing their abilities.

However, when they first came in (during different years), I looked at each one to see what he had and then said to myself, "Oh gracious, if he can make a real contribution, a *playing* contribution, to our team then we must be pretty lousy." However, what I couldn't see was what these men had inside.

Both of them worked so hard to bring out their best. They gave me—and more importantly, the team—very close to everything they could possibly give.

Conrad Burke became a starter for two and a half years; Doug McIntosh became our starting center and played on a national championship team.

You may not have heard of them, but each epitomizes what I define as success in an individual. They came close to making the most of their God-given talent.

Perceptions of Success

I'm perceived as a very successful basketball coach because of the ten national championships UCLA won while I was there. But I know of coaches I consider every bit as capable as I am—better, in fact—who never won a national championship, never even came close. Did they fail as coaches?

In the first fourteen years I coached at UCLA we didn't win a national championship, even though I worked every bit as hard as in those years as when we won ten of them.

Did I fail as a coach during the first fourteen years? Was I a success only when I coached a team that won a national championship?

Zero National Championships

If UCLA had never won a national championship while I was coaching there, I would still have considered myself very successful because I was judging myself on other things, things I had some control over. For example, how hard am I trying to produce the very best team we can possibly be?

Had we not won any championships, I would have been disappointed, yes, but still a success in my own eyes. I would have had peace of mind because of the effort I put forth.

The ten national titles provided no additional peace of mind nor sense of validation of my efforts as a coach. That I already had. I had succeeded long before I was called a success.

Failure Is Not Fatal, But Failure to Change Might Be

Failure to change is often just stubbornness that comes from an unwillingness to learn, an inability to realize that you're not perfect. There cannot be progress without change—even though not all change is progress.

My rule regarding UCLA's dress code for travel changed with the times. Initially I insisted on a coat and tie, dress slacks, and polished shoes for an overall clean-cut appearance.

Eventually I came to understand that the culture had changed. Ideas of what constituted appropriate dress had changed, and the coat and tie were viewed as only one possibility by many people I respected.

I realized the fundamental issue was not specifically a coat or a tie, dress slacks, or polished shoes. The issue was overall appearance. To me a clean-cut appearance was important for team image and self-image. I told athletes if they could accomplish that without a coat and tie, fine.

Eventually my dress code required only that they have a clean-cut appearance when we traveled. That remained because it was important. I came to believe a tie in itself wasn't the important issue, and I changed my rule.

Big-Money Players and Coaches

Coaches are paid millions of dollars today and players make tens of millions of dollars. It started happening soon after I left UCLA, so I'm often asked if I'm envious. Folks say, "Coach Wooden, imagine what you could make today!"

It doesn't concern me in the least. What concerns me is that over which I have some measure of control and I can't control what others make or employers pay them. However, I can control whether or not I worry about it. And I don't.

I have no say over how much somebody chooses to pay Shaquille O'Neal or anyone else. In fact, I'm happy if someone can earn that amount of money. It's completely out of hand, but they have a right to take what is offered.

It's simple. Don't compare yourself to somebody else, especially materially. If I'm worrying about the other guy and what he's doing, about what he's making, about all the attention he's getting, I'm not going to be able to do what I'm capable of doing. It's a guaranteed way to make yourself miserable.

Envy, jealousy, and criticism can become cancerous. They hurt the person who feels them rather than the person they're directed toward.

If I'm envious of how much Mr. O'Neal or a coach is paid, is that going to hurt him in any way? Of course not. It's going to hurt me.

He may know what it's like to earn a million dollars, but I know what it was like to be able to get a good meal for twenty-five cents. Neither of us should envy the other in this regard.

Adversity Makes You Stronger

Most all good things come through adversity. There's a poem that says:

Looking back it seems to me,
All the grief that had to be
Left me when the pain was o'er
Stronger than I was before.
—*Unknown*

I believe that. We get stronger when we test ourselves. Adversity can make us better. We must be challenged to improve, and adversity is the challenger.

Character Creates Longevity

I believe ability can get you to the top, but it takes character to keep you there. A big part of character is the self-discipline needed to avoid complacency, resist temptation, and understand that past success doesn't guarantee future success.

It's so easy to relax, to cut corners, to let down after you've reached your goal, and begin thinking you can just "turn it on" automatically, without proper preparation. It takes real character to keep working as hard or even harder once you're there.

When you read about an athlete or team that wins over and over and over, remind yourself, "More than ability, they have character."

Remember this your lifetime through—
Tomorrow, there will be more to do.
And failure waits for all who stay

With some success made yesterday.
Tomorrow, you must try once more
And even harder than before.

Kareem Learns from Adversity

When the rules committee outlawed the dunk after the 1966–67 season, I supported it because I didn't think that shot was good for the game. I still feel that way. However, Kareem disagreed. He thought the rule change was aimed directly at him.

In fact, though I don't know if this was true, I felt the change was directed at the Houston players. They would frequently hang on the rim, actually bend it, during the warm-up. When we played them in '67, crews had to come out with ladders to straighten it out before our game got under way.

Whatever the source of the rules change, Kareem would no longer able to stuff the ball without being penalized, and he was unhappy.

I told him, "Lewis, this will make you a better player. You'll have to work harder developing your hook shot, the little short shots off the boards, and the shots around the basket. There is no way this will do anything but make you a much better ballplayer."

He nodded. And then I added, "Lewis, remember when you get to the pros, you won't have forgotten how to dunk."

When Kareem became a professional, one of his most feared shots was the skyhook, a shot he had developed and perfected after the rule change. He had faced a challenge and used it to strengthen himself. Adversity can do that, but it needs your assistance.

Persistence Is Stronger than Failure

Abraham Lincoln is acknowledged as one of America's greatest presidents. Here is a brief summary of his career:

Failed in business	1831
Defeated for legislature	1832
Failed in business again	1833
Elected to legislature	1834
Sweetheart died	1835
Had nervous breakdown	1836
Defeated for speaker	1838
Defeated for elector	1840
Defeated for congressional nomination	1843
Elected to Congress	1846
Defeated for Congress	1848
Defeated for Senate	1855
Defeated for Vice President	1856
Defeated for Senate	1859
Elected President of the United States	1860

Few people have suffered more personal, professional, and political adversity than Abraham Lincoln. He persisted in the face of failure and emerged victorious.

Another president, Calvin Coolidge, described it very well:

> Nothing in the world can take the place of persistence. Talent will not; nothing is more common than unsuccessful men with talent. Genius will not; unrewarded genius is almost a proverb. Education will not; the world is full of educated derelicts. Persistence and determination alone are omnipotent.

The model Mr. Lincoln gave us with his persistence is one we can remember in the face of our own setbacks. And what is most wondrous of all is that persistence is a quality that we ourselves control. You, and only you, can decide whether you will stay the course.

Always Be Progressing

You must never stand still. You're either moving upward a little bit or you're going the other way. You can't expect to go upward too quickly, but you can sure go down very quickly.

The slide down happens in a hurry. Progress comes slowly but steadily if you are patient and prepare diligently.

Every member of every UCLA basketball team who ever played and practiced with us will tell you that one of my most common expressions was "Move, move, move!" I meant it both physically *and* mentally.

The India Rubber Man

My nickname when I was a basketball player at Purdue was the India Rubber Man because when I was knocked down I would immediately bounce right back up and keep playing. In the team photograph from 1931, I'm the only player with bandages on both knees.

I've always believed that hustle can make up for a lot of mistakes.

Balance in Basketball (and Life)

Balance is perhaps the most important word for a player or coach to keep in mind. You have to have emotional balance. You have to have physical balance. You have to have mental balance. As coach I had to teach players individual balance, and then the balance of losing themselves in the group for the greater good of the team.

Balance means keeping things in proper perspective, not permitting either excessive exuberance or dejection to interfere with preparation, performance, or subsequent individual or team behavior.

Balance is important in many aspects of basketball. Besides physical, emotional, and mental balance, we need squad balance, rebounding balance, offensive balance, defensive balance, size balance. Balance. Balance. Balance.

The same thing is true in life. We must have physical, emotional, and mental balance; balance between making a living and making a home. We must keep things in perspective, both the good and the bad.

And we must listen to achieve that balance. Listen and observe at home and work. Balance the work against the play.

Achieving balance in life (or basketball) requires great, great effort, desire, and alertness. Life is complicated, and it's easy to get things totally out of balance. That's when you have a problem.

The Importance of Basketball

Basketball is just a game, but if I was doing my job as a coach that game of basketball would help our players by preparing them to do well in life, to reach their full potential as individuals.

When they did that, I felt very proud as a coach. That's more rewarding to me than all the championships and titles and awards.

I'm asked, "Coach, aren't you particularly proud of all the players that went on to the pros after they left UCLA, fellows like Bill Walton, Kareem Abdul-Jabbar, Sidney

Wicks, Gail Goodrich, David Meyers, Lucius Allen, Mike Warren, Keith Erickson, Walt Hazzard, Henry Bibby, Marques Johnson, and the others?"

Yes, but I'm equally proud of the fellows who became doctors, lawyers, dentists, ministers, businessmen, teachers, and coaches.

The coach whose philosophy I have admired as much as any coach I've ever been associated with is Amos Alonzo Stagg. He was coaching football at the University of Chicago when they were a national power. After one very successful year a reporter said, "Coach Stagg, it was a great year! A really great year."

Coach Stagg said, "I won't know for another twenty years or so whether you're correct."

He meant that it would take that long to see how the youngsters under his supervision turned out in life.

That's how I feel. I'm most proud of the athlete who does well with his life. That's where success is. Basketball is just a very small part of it.

The Olympics: Good and Not So Good

There are two Olympics: the Special Olympics and the Olympic Games.

I support the Special Olympics. My goodness, there you'll witness what the spirit of the game is all about. You'll see the thrill on the face of a competitor who comes in last but gives it absolutely everything he or she has! They prepare hard. They compete hard. They succeed even with a last-place finish. This is a lesson with real depth.

I no longer feel that supportive of the Olympic Games, which have become almost professional. You'll see an athlete complaining about coming in second because he knows it will cost him in endorsements. Going for the gold has too often become going for the green.

The Final Score

The "final score" is not the final score. My final score is how *prepared* you were to execute near your own particular level of competence, both individually and as a team.

There is nothing wrong with that other fellow being better than you are, as long as you did everything you possibly could to prepare yourself for the competition. That is all you have control over. That is all you should concern yourself with. It may be that the other fellow's level of competency is simply higher than yours. That doesn't make you a loser.

In 1962 in the Final Four against Cincinnati (who won the championship that year), we lost in the last few seconds of our semifinal game. However, Walter Hazzard, Gary Cunningham, Peter Blackman, John Green, Fred

Slaughter, and the other UCLA players left the court as winners in my eyes.

I was disappointed that we lost, of course, but I had the greatest pride in how the team had performed and how they had prepared hard and progressed during the year.

We were almost 20 points down in the first ten minutes of the game and then came from behind to even it up at the half. We fought very hard in the second half and Cincinnati perhaps had superior personnel.

But what I saw out on the court during that game was a UCLA team that came as close as we could come to being the best that we could be. That's a wonderful accomplishment! Goodness gracious sakes, am I proud of that effort. So proud, even now.

Was I disappointed we were outscored? I am *still* disappointed we were outscored—but I was never dejected. Mostly what I was, and am, is proud. Our team was outscored, but we were winners. I had the greatest pride in how the players prepared, progressed, and performed.

I felt this philosophy would have a much greater positive impact on the outcome of events than a stress on trying to outscore opponents. It's a focus on improving yourself rather than comparing yourself to the other team as indicated by a score.

Furthermore, when you get too engrossed in those things over which you have no control, it will adversely affect those things over which you *do* have control—namely, your preparation.

You respect everyone. Then you simply make the strongest effort to prepare to the fullest extent of your abilities. The result will take care of itself, and you should be willing to accept it.

The Glory Is in Getting There

When people ask me now if I miss coaching UCLA basketball games, the national championships, the attention, the trophies, and everything that goes with them, I tell them this: I miss the practices.

I don't miss the games or the tournaments or all the other folderol. As Robert Louis Stevenson wrote, "It is better to travel hopefully than arrive." I tried to do that.

It's the practices I miss most even now.

PART III

COACHING, TEACHING, LEADING

In great attempts it is glorious even to fail.

—WILFRED A. PETERSON

A Sacred Trust

A leader, particularly a teacher or coach, has a most powerful influence on those he or she leads, perhaps more than anyone outside of the family. Therefore, it is the obligation of that leader, teacher, or coach to treat such responsibility as a grave concern.

I consider it a sacred trust: helping to mold character, instill productive principles and values, and provide a positive example to those under my supervision.

Furthermore, it is a privilege to have that responsibility, opportunity, and obligation, one that should never be taken lightly.

Philosophers and Prison Guards

Mr. Webster indicates that, among other things, a philosopher is a person who meets all events, whether favorable or unfavorable, with calmness and composure.

A philosopher is also one who has a love of wisdom, studies the general principles of a field of knowledge or activity, and the processes governing thought, conduct, character, morals, and behavior.

I believe these same traits are inherent in a leader. A real leader is much more than simply a person with authority.

A prison guard has authority, but he or she is not a leader. A leader doesn't need a gun to motivate individuals.

Who Can Lead?

Leadership is the ability to get individuals to work together for the common good and the best possible results while at the same time letting them know they did it themselves.

Some people are automatic leaders. Some can never be leaders. But many who don't think of themselves as leaders have the potential to become such if they understand the fundamentals of getting individuals to work together.

Those fundamentals can be learned. I learned them.

"But, Coach Wooden, Times Have Changed!"

"There was a time when the vast majority would follow blindly, even into the shadow of death, but such is not the case now. Young people of today are far more aware, inclined to be more openly critical and more genuinely inquisitive than they used to be. So leaders must work with them somewhat differently."

I wrote the preceding observation more than a quarter of a century ago.

Are people *really* that different today? Have times changed so much? I wonder about that.

"Why Did Wooden Win?"

There is no area of basketball in which I am a genius. None. Tactically and strategically I'm just average, and this is not offering false modesty.

We won national championships while I was coaching at UCLA because I was above average in analyzing players, getting them to fill roles as part of a *team*, paying attention to fundamentals and details, and working well with others, both those under my supervision and those whose supervision I was under. Additionally, I enjoyed very hard work.

There is nothing fancy about these qualities. They have wide application and equal effectiveness in any team endeavor anywhere. If there is any mystery as to why UCLA won ten national championships while I was the coach, that may clear it up.

A Leader's Difficult Task

A person in a position of leadership must make decisions. Making decisions is a tough job. Those under a leader can make suggestions. Making suggestions is an easy job.

Everybody has a suggestion. Not everybody has a decision.

Perhaps that's why there are so few leaders—at least, good leaders.

Respect

The most essential thing for a leader to have is the respect of those under his or her supervision. It starts with giving them respect.

You must make it clear that you are working together. Those under your supervision are not working for you but with you, and you all have a common goal.

Remember, you can have respect for a person without necessarily liking that individual. Coach Amos Alonzo Stagg said, "I loved all my players. I didn't like them all, but I did love them all." What does that mean?

You love your children, but you may not like some of the things they do. We are instructed, "Love thy neighbor as thyself." That doesn't mean we have to like everything our neighbor does. That has nothing to do with our love for them.

You must have respect, which is a part of love, for those under your supervision. Then they will do what you ask and more. They'll go the extra distance, make the extra effort in trying to accomplish the most they can within the framework of the team.

If they don't respect their leader, people just punch the clock in and out. There is no clock-watching when a leader has respect.

A Leader Is Fair

Fairness is giving all people the treatment they *earn* and deserve. It doesn't mean treating everyone alike. That's unfair, because everyone doesn't earn the same treatment.

That's why I didn't treat all players alike. I didn't treat Walter Hazzard like I treated Gail Goodrich. I didn't treat Bill Walton like I treated Keith Wilkes. Contrary to what you might think, it enhanced teamwork, because almost every player I coached knew that he would be treated *fairly*, that he would be given exactly what he had earned and deserved. They worked harder as a result. It's true in sports and elsewhere in life.

In all circumstances, whether as a coach, teacher, or business leader, you must begin by determining exactly what is fair. That means you must eliminate prejudice of all types. Can you do it 100 percent? Probably not, but you can try.

Those under you will recognize that you at least are making a sincere effort. They will realize that you will be wrong on occasion. They must understand, as must you, that you are imperfect. But as long as those under your supervision know that you are trying hard to be fair, you'll do fine—whether it's with your children, employees, or athletes.

Walk the Walk

A leader's most powerful ally is his or her own example. Leaders don't just talk about doing something; they do it. Swen Nater, a former player at UCLA, told me once, "Coach, you walked the walk." He meant that I led by example.

Pride as a Motivator

Pride is a better motivator than fear. I never wanted to teach through fear, punishment, or intimidation.

Fear may work in the short term to get people to do something, but over the long run I believe personal pride is a much greater motivator. It produces far better results that last for a much longer time.

Who would I prefer to work with, an individual who has great personal pride or one who is fearful of punishment? That's an easy choice for me.

Remember, pride comes when you give respect.

Dictator Leaders

Abraham Lincoln said, "Most anyone can stand adversity, but to test a person's character give him power."

I believe there was a difference between General George S. Patton and General Omar Bradley. General Bradley had a great concern for those under his supervision. He knew what had to be done and he wasn't looking for self-glory.

If you saw the movie *Patton*, you saw a man who acted as a dictator. While I would want him on my side in time of war, I believe we should lead athletes and associates in a different manner.

There are coaches out there who have won championships with a dictator approach, among them Vince Lombardi and Bobby Knight. I had a different philosophy. I didn't want to be a dictator to my players or assistant coaches or managers. For me, concern, compassion, and consideration were always priorities of the highest order.

Leaders Listen

Listen to those under your supervision. Really listen. Don't act as though you're listening and let it go in one ear and out the other. Faking it is worse than not doing it at all.

A good motto is "Others, too, have brains."

Another Golden Rule

Reward individuals for things well done. It doesn't have to be in a material way. Sometimes a pat on the back is more meaningful in many ways than something material. A smile. A nod.

Leadership and Punishment

Leaders have to discipline. Those who dispense discipline must remember that its purpose is to help, to prevent, to correct, to improve, rather than to punish. You are not likely to get productive results if you antagonize. Punishment antagonizes.

Furthermore, it is important to understand the purpose of criticism. Criticism is not meant to punish, but rather to correct something that is preventing better results. The *only* goal of criticism or discipline is improvement. You must keep that in mind and try to the best of your ability to use tact.

Public Embarrassment

I feel that hard public criticism embarrasses people, antagonizes them, and may discourage them from being receptive to your message. It is counterproductive, whether it's on a basketball court or in a business establishment.

Occasionally it can be a useful tool, however. One player (and I will *not* embarrass him by using his name) needed to be goaded publicly. I had to make him mad at me at times, until he was determined that he was really going to show me. However, such public embarrassment is very rarely useful.

The Worst Punishment of All

The worst punishment I could give a team was to deny participation in what was very hard work. I wanted my players to understand that practicing together on our UCLA basketball team was indeed a privilege, a privilege that could be taken away from them.

If they weren't working hard in practice I would say, "Well, fellows, let's call it off for today. We're just not with it."

The vast majority of the time the players would immediately say, "Coach, give us another chance. We'll get going." Usually that was all it would take, the threat of taking away their privilege of practicing. Keep in mind that our practices were physically and mentally grueling.

On rare occasions when that didn't work, when the players continued to coast, I would simply terminate the practice session, turn out the lights, and leave.

The privilege of practicing had been taken away. It was the worst punishment of all: "Gentlemen, practice is over."

False Expectations

When *Sports Illustrated* came out with its poll each year saying UCLA was going to be number one in the nation again, what did it mean?

I told our players to remember that that poll was just somebody else's opinion, their guess. *Sports Illustrated* doesn't know what's going to happen in the future, and if you let yourself believe it, you're in trouble because you will have false expectations.

The so-called experts are basing their opinion on the past, and if you try getting by on that, you're in trouble. Yesterday's gone. It'll never change. What you do *today* will determine what's going to happen tomorrow, not what you did yesterday; certainly not a poll—somebody else's *guess* about what's going to happen tomorrow.

Here's the only expectation it is useful to have in your mind, regardless of your profession: "I will do the best I am capable of doing today to bring out my best tomorrow." Now you have an expectation that is productive.

Scouting

I seldom mentioned the other team. I believe it takes away from the concentration on ourselves in the preparation.

I did less scouting than any other coach I've ever heard about. I wanted our team to concentrate on what we could do—namely, try to execute our style of play to the best of our abilities.

Of course, I needed to know something about the opponent in general terms, but I could read that in a newspaper.

I would know their overall characteristics, such as who was the coach and what was their style so we could be prepared to attack their 2–2–1, or their 1–2–2, or their 3–1–1, or whatever they had. However, I didn't want to talk much about that with my players.

I felt we were better off letting our opponents try to figure us out than spending time trying to figure them out. We focused on preparing for any eventuality rather than a particular style of play from a particular team. What if we prepared for something specific and our opponent changed? Uh-oh.

Perhaps we gained an advantage by having so much confidence in our own ability to play near our potential (because of our detailed and disciplined preparation) that it kept us from becoming fearful of another team.

It goes back to focusing on what you can control. We had no control over the many possible variations an opponent might use in a game. We did have control, total control, over preparing to execute our game. To me, it made more sense to concentrate on that.

Psychological Warfare

I was disinclined to play so-called mind games with opponents. However, there was one idea I used that was aimed directly at the opponents' physiology as well as their psychology.

Never did I want to call the first time-out during a game. Never. It was almost a fetish with me because I stressed conditioning to such a degree. I wanted UCLA to come out and run our opponents so hard that they would be forced to call the first time-out just to catch their breath. I wanted them to have to stop the running before we did.

At that first time-out, the opponent would know, and we would know they knew, who was in better condition.

This has a psychological impact.

Leadership Is More than Facts

There is very little difference in technical knowledge about the game of basketball among most experienced coaches. Similarly, in the business world, those in charge usually understand the basics: how to read a financial statement and so forth.

However, there is a vast difference between leaders in their ability to teach and to motivate those under their supervision.

Knowledge alone is not enough to get desired results. You must have the more elusive ability to teach and to motivate. This defines a leader; if you can't teach and you can't motivate, you can't lead.

Wilt Teaches Me a Lesson

When Wilt Chamberlain was traded to the Los Angeles Lakers many years ago, I was invited to the press conference. One of the reporters asked him this question. "Wilt, do you think Coach Van Breda Kolff (the Lakers' coach) can handle you? It's been said you're hard to handle."

Wilt replied, "You 'handle' farm animals. You work with people. I am a person. I can work with anyone."

I realized he was absolutely right; the term "handle" was inappropriate. Furthermore, I realized that two days earlier my book on teaching and coaching the techniques of basketball, *Practical Modern Basketball*, had been published with a section called "Handling Your Players." I understood that needed to be corrected immediately.

I rushed home and called the publisher that same day and explained my desire to change the heading and text as soon as possible from "handling your players" to "working with your players."

Mr. Chamberlain was correct. I believe that a leader and those under his or her supervision are working together. The former doesn't "handle" the latter. For that reason I did not refer to UCLA as "my team" or the athletes as "my players." And after hearing Wilt's comment, I never again referred to "handling players." You may try to handle a couple of mules like Jack and Kate back on Dad's farm, but it's the wrong attitude to apply to those you work with.

It's a subtle difference, but it all adds up in the bigger picture of good leadership.

Emotionalism

I believe that for every artificial peak you create, there is a valley. I don't like valleys. Games are lost in valleys. Therefore, I wasn't much for giving speeches to stir up emotions before a game.

If you need emotionalism to make you perform better, then sooner or later you'll be vulnerable, an emotional wreck, and unable to function to your level of ability.

My ideal is an ever-rising graph line that peaks with your final performance.

I prefer thorough preparation over some device to make us "rise to the occasion." Let others try to rise suddenly to a higher level than they had attained previously. We would have already attained it in our preparation. We would be there to begin with. A speech by me shouldn't be necessary.

Hatred

Hatred motivates only briefly. It is a variation of rage or anger and is a result of emotionalism. Emotions aren't lasting. When emotions take over, reason flies out the window and prevents you from functioning near your level of competency. Mistakes occur when your thinking is tainted by excessive emotion.

You may refute that in a sense by saying that love is an emotion and it is productive. But isn't it true that when you're in love, really in love, your ability to reason may be somewhat reduced? Of course, I can only speak for myself on that issue.

Generally, to perform near your level of competency your mind must be clear and free of excessive emotions, such as hatred.

Unless you're attempting to run through a brick wall, excessive emotion is counterproductive.

When to Be Dejected

You are entitled to be dejected when you know you didn't do what you should have done in preparing yourself to execute near your own ability level. Yes, then you have reason to be dejected.

But if you have prepared yourself properly, there is no reason to be downhearted. Disappointed perhaps, but not excessively so.

The most disappointing thing that happened to me in basketball was losing the final game of the Indiana state high school championship by one single point. That was back in 1928 at Butler Field House in Indianapolis. We lost to Muncie Central 13–12 in the last seconds of the game on a shot that seemed to clear the rafters before it finally went through the basket.

When the buzzer signaled the end of that game, one that is still talked about by old-time Indiana basketball fans, most of my teammates broke down and cried. I did not. I believed I had done the best I could. I had prepared and played hard and knew it.

The team had prepared and played hard. I saw no reason to be overly distressed because we had lost a game, even a championship game. I wasn't. Disappointed, of course, but not overly dejected and downhearted.

I felt even then that the more important question was, "Did I try to do all I could?" rather than "Did I win?" If the answer to the first question was, yes, then the answer to the second question was also, yes, regardless of the score.

There is nothing to be ashamed of when you prepared to the best of your ability. But you have ample cause to be dejected when you know you didn't prepare properly when you had the ability to do so.

Jubilation

There's nothing wrong with jubilation. It's excessive jubilation that I cautioned against: showboating, hotdogging, conducting yourself in a fashion that is simply a display of arrogance, behaving in an egotistical sort of way.

The year before we lost the championship game to Muncie Central in the 1928 Indiana state high school tournament, we had won the title. Then, too, I saw no reason to be overly jubilant—though I was very happy, of course.

It's important to keep things in perspective. When they get out of perspective, it affects your ability to prepare and perform. It harms your peace of mind.

Spiking, Dunking, Taunting, Flaunting

Today's showboating runs contrary to what the spirit of the game is all about. Excessive dunking, pointing at other players, and taunting them, all belittle your opponent and show a lack of respect.

I believe you should go out and work hard, play hard, and compete hard in sports and in life without the extra histrionics.

We played ten times for the national championship while I was coaching at UCLA. Each time we were fortunate enough to win. And each time near the end of the contest when I felt we had the game in hand, I told the team during a time-out, "Now, remember when this game is over to behave in an appropriate manner. Do not make fools of yourselves. Let the alumni and student body do that if they choose. Don't you do it!"

Your reaction to victory or defeat is an important part of how you play the game. I wanted my players to display style and class in either situation—to lose with grace, to win with humility.

A Coach's Best Friend

I used the bench to teach. When future two-time All-American Walter Hazzard first came to us at UCLA, he had a tendency to get a little fancy. He didn't continue being fancy because he liked to play. Early on we may have lost a couple of games because I sat him on the bench for being too fancy.

I tell coaches at coaching clinics, "The greatest ally you have to get things working well and players performing as a team is the bench. Don't be afraid to use it, whether for a star player or anyone else. In fact, the overall effect can be better when you bench a star. The other players see it and play harder because of it."

Even if there is a price to be paid, don't be afraid to use appropriate discipline. It may hurt in the short term, but it will pay dividends in the future.

Sports as Teacher

Sports show us so clearly how to work together with others to get the best results. They show that you must think of the group as a whole rather than just of yourself as an individual.

I often used the comparison of a movie or stage play. One great actor or actress isn't enough. You must have supporting players if it's going to become a great motion picture: not only other actors and actresses (some of whom may not even have speaking roles), but also lighting people, scriptwriters, makeup artists, camera operators, grips, musicians, and everyone else. You need a director and a producer.

And the important thing I wanted my players to understand was that just as a movie needs a variety of individuals *all* working very hard for the good of the movie, a basketball team needs a variety of individuals all working very hard for the good of the group.

We've seen many motion pictures where the star did a terrific job but the movie was a failure. I wanted every member of our basketball team to understand that the goal was to make ourselves into the best team we could possibly be, not to create a star.

Of course, the one who has to understand that the most is often the so-called star.

Being Prepared

I used to say to an individual player who was unhappy because he wanted more playing time, "Young man, tell yourself, 'I will be prepared and then perhaps my chance will come, because if it does come and I'm not ready, another chance may not come my way very soon again.'"

The time to prepare isn't after you have been given the opportunity. It's long before that opportunity arises. Once the opportunity arrives, it's too late to prepare.

The Guaranteed Dividend

I believe one of the big lessons of sports for dedicated individuals and teams is that it shows us how hard work, and I mean *hard* work, does pay dividends.

The dividend is not *necessarily* in outscoring an opponent. The guaranteed dividend is the complete peace of mind gained in knowing you did everything within your power, physically, mentally, and emotionally, to bring forth your full potential.

I see the same self-satisfaction occurring in every area of our lives when we strive mightily to do our best, whether it's working in a business or community or raising a family.

The great satisfaction that comes from trying to do your best is the guaranteed dividend.

Tex Schramm's Point

Former Dallas Cowboys general manager Tex Schramm said, "Sports is not just about winning. It's about winning with style and class. That was the old Cowboys. It was the old Celtics. The old Yankees. They were something special. Now all I see that matters is results."

I agree with Mr. Schramm. I was a great Cowboy fan when Tom Landry was there. And Roger Staubach. I am not a great Cowboy fan now because the emphasis shifted to just winning and it didn't seem to matter how you won or how you behaved in winning. It's the slogan of the Oakland Raiders: "Just win, baby." They're more concerned with the end than the means. To me, the means is very important.

Owners and Profits

Team owners nowadays will say, "This is a business. I need to turn a profit." However, for many of them owning a team is really just a hobby. If they're smart enough to become multimultimillionaires in business, they're going to make more money staying in business than getting into professional sports.

When sports becomes just a business, it loses something intrinsic to its spirit. The spirit of the game is a beautiful thing.

Bringing Out Your Best
(Whatever It Is)

As a player at Purdue University I had not been blessed
with height or size. Those were things over which I had
no control. But the Good Lord had given me quickness
and speed, and those were things over which I had some
control. I focused on them with great intensity. I worked
very hard on conditioning for quickness and speed.

When I graduated, Coach Piggy Lambert said I was
the best-conditioned athlete he had ever seen in any sport.
I had worked at it—at what I had control over.

Later, I applied the same philosophy to our teams:
focus all your effort on what is within your power to control. Conditioning is one of those things. How your mind
functions is another.

The Gym Is a Classroom

I felt that running a practice session was almost like teaching an English class in that I wanted to have a lesson
plan. I knew the detailed plan was necessary in teaching
English, but it took a while before I understood the same
thing was necessary in sports. Otherwise you waste an
enormous amount of time, effort, and talent.

I would spend almost as much time planning a practice as conducting it. Everything was listed on three-by-five cards down to the very last detail.

Everything was planned out each day. In fact, in my later years at UCLA I would spend two hours every morning with my assistants organizing that day's practice session (even though the practice itself might be less than two hours long). I kept a record of every practice session in a looseleaf notebook for future reference.

My coaches and managers also had three-by-five cards each day so they knew—to the exact minute—when we would need two basketballs at one end of the court for a drill, or five basketballs at midcourt for a different drill, or three players against two players at a certain place and time, or the dozens and dozens of variations I devised.

I kept notes with the specifics of every minute of every hour of every practice we ever had at UCLA. When I planned a day's practice, I looked back to see what we'd done on the corresponding day the previous year and the year before that.

By doing that I could track the practice routines of every single player for every single practice session he participated in while I was coaching him. In those days freshmen were ineligible. Otherwise I would have gone back three years in reviewing the drills.

It was very important that I learn about each player and then study that player so I would know if he needed a little more time on this or that particular drill. I needed to know which drill had greater application to this player or that player, because individuals vary.

So I devised drills for both individuals and the group and studied and analyzed them. Some drills would be good for all and some drills would be good for just certain players.

I needed to understand how to apply these drills in practice. I learned I must not continue them too long. I must know as the season progressed how they were going to change and then devise new ones to prevent monotony, although there would be some drills we must do every single day of the year.

All those things I had a responsibility to do to the utmost of my ability because they were things over which I had control.

The attention to detail meant players would move quickly from one drill to another. We didn't achieve conditioning by doing laps or running up and down stairs or doing push-ups. We did it through the efficient and intense execution of individual fundamental drills.

A shooting drill was a conditioning drill the way I ran it. There was no standing around and just watching or resting in between. The players were always working and running and moving. "Move! Move! Move! Up, back, up, back, move. Quickly, hurry up!"

A player who wasn't running in a scrimmage would shoot free throws until he had made ten in a row and then would go into the scrimmage while someone else came out to shoot free throws. Everyone wanted to be scrimmaging, so players put tremendous pressure on themselves to make free throws and worked intensely while they participated in the scrimmage. "Move! Move! Move!" No resting. No standing around. No idle chatter.

The pressure I created during practices may have exceeded that which opponents produced. I believe when an individual constantly works under pressure, he or she will respond automatically when faced with it during competition.

I engaged in very little discussion. I'd talk while drills were going on, mostly to individuals rather than to the group. I did more individual coaching in that sense.

Following the drills, I would make notes. Perhaps we needed two more minutes on this drill or less time to complete that drill.

By reviewing and analyzing everything, we were able to get the very most out of our practice time. That was necessary to reach our goal: getting the very most out of our abilities.

Then I would say, "Young men, you have a responsibility for the attainment and 'maintainment' of all the little details that we do in practice. Your responsibility begins each afternoon when practice ends, because you can tear down more between practices than we can possibly build up during practices. So please practice moderation in what you do."

But it all began with attention to, and perfection of, details. Details. Details.

Develop a love for details. They usually accompany success.

Love of the Routine

Some people wondered how I could endure working in such a minutely detailed, persistent, and arduous manner day after day, week after week, for years on end. I could tell them only this: "I love it." It was as Cervantes described. For me the journey *was* the inn.

The practice and the planning and the drills were my journey, and I loved it.

The Crowd Loves Blood

I worked at the Indianapolis 500 when I was teaching and coaching in Indiana. People used to clamor for seats on the south turn. They would pay a premium to sit there. Why? That's where most of the accidents were. No accidents? Dull race.

People go to a boxing match and the bout is beautifully and scientifically fought but there's no knockout. No blood. Afterward, fans will tell you it was a dull fight.

Athletes increasingly play to this crowd instinct with hotdogging and showmanship. It's unnecessary and it loses the spirit of the game.

Flash Versus Class

Youngsters watch professionals and see that it's OK to showboat and belittle opponents. I believe performing with style and class is a first priority, especially if you're in the public spotlight. If you're in that position, you do have a responsibility.

That's why it's sad to hear someone like Charles Barkley say he's not interested in being a role model for anyone. When you get into a profession that puts you in the limelight you have accepted that responsibility. It comes with the job.

Maybe I'm old-fashioned, but that's the way I look at it. And I'm not likely to change.

Role Models: Good and Bad

Tony Gwynn, Steve Young, Jerry Rice, Chris Evert, Emmett Smith, Cal Ripken Jr., Jack Nicklaus, Jackie

Joyner-Kersee, Pete Sampras, Wayne Gretsky, John Stockton, David Robinson, Akeem Olajuwon, and Kevin Johnson are outstanding examples for us of athletes with great style and class. I'm speaking both of their playing and conduct in the competitive arena and of what they're doing with their lives and for their communities. They are wonderful role models.

Michael Jordan has showmanship on the court, but it seems to be a natural part of his exuberance and energy and love of the game. He avoids "in your face" stuff.

As great a player as Dennis Rodman is, and he is a *great* player, I wouldn't want him on a team. He is an egotist with a great desire to attract attention. I don't think he realizes that his tremendous individual abilities will attract all the attention that anyone could want. And it will be the right kind of attention.

Spirit Versus Temperament

There is a difference between spirit and termperament. It is a slight difference, but it is an important one. I valued players with spirit and avoided those who were temperamental.

Keith Erickson had spirit without being temperamental. At times he would test me to the limit. He was playful but not mean. He had fun without trying to be funny.

Keith would watch me out of the corner of his eye and when he thought I wasn't looking engage in a bit of horseplay, such as seeing how far and how high he could throw the ball from one end of the court to the other. He was not disruptive, just spirited.

More important, he brought that spirit into the competitive situation. The tougher the job I assigned him in a game, the more he gave of himself. He had tremendous fight in him.

Gail Goodrich was another player who was spirited, a fighter, but never temperamental. Spirit is good. Temperament is bad. A leader is charged with recognizing the difference.

The Value in Feeling Valued

The individuals who aren't playing much have a very important role in the development of those who are going to play more. They are needed, and you must let them know it.

Everyone on the team, from the manager to the coach, from a secretary to an owner, has a role to fulfill. That role is valuable if the team is to come close to reaching its potential. The leader must understand this.

Every single member of your team needs to feel wanted and appreciated. If they are on the team, they *deserve* to be valued and to feel valued. Do you want someone on the team who doesn't feel necessary and appreciated? How do they find out unless you let them know?

Right after each UCLA basketball game, there would be a press conference with representatives from all the media. I could predict what questions they would ask and which players they wanted to interview.

I always tried to use this opportunity to praise those individuals the media would overlook. I would say, "When I put so-and-so in just before the half and he made that steal, it quite possibly could have been the turning point in the game." I wanted to let other players know they were very important to the team.

The press would give plenty of attention and praise to so-called stars: Bill Walton, Kareem Abdul-Jabbar, Gail Goodrich, Walter Hazzard, Sidney Wicks, Marques Johnson, David Meyers, and others. I would be more likely to praise these particular players privately.

I wanted the public acknowledgment for players to be balanced. The average basketball fan may have been unfamiliar with names like Neville Saner, Bill Sweek, or Gary Franklin, fellows who were an important part of UCLA teams.

I tried to let them know they were important, that they were valued. All members of the team are important. Each role is so crucial.

In *Elegy Written in a Country Churchyard*, Thomas Gray wrote,

Full many a gem of purest ray serene,
The dark unfathomed caves of ocean bear:
Full many a flower is born to blush unseen,
And waste its sweetness on the desert air.

The star knows he's important and hears it from a variety of sources. You must make sure that others on the team, those "born to blush unseen," understand that their role is also very, very important. They should never feel their efforts are wasted in the star's shadow.

It's up to the leader to do that, in sports and elsewhere.

Swen Nater Understood His Role

Swen Nater was playing basketball at Cypress Junior College in Southern California when I spoke to him about coming to UCLA. He was nearly seven feet tall and had an outstanding physique, although his basketball skills were somewhat limited because he had spent his early years in Holland.

I told him, "Swen, if you come to UCLA you will play very little in actual games, maybe not at all because I've got someone coming in who is extremely talented." The player coming in was Bill Walton.

"However," I continued, "if you work with us, practice with and against this player, by the time you graduate

I feel certain that you'll get a pro contract. You'll be that good because of the role you'll play on our team."

Swen listened and joined us. He understood his role. The first year he hardly challenged Bill. The second year he made great progress. The third year he gave Bill Walton all he could handle.

Swen knew his individual role and his team role and never once complained. As a result, everyone benefited: the UCLA basketball team as a group, Bill Walton as an individual, and Swen Nater, who, after graduation, joined San Diego in the ABA (the old American Basketball Association) and became rookie of the year.

110 Percent Isn't the Goal

The players were charged with trying to improve a little each day, trying to get closer to becoming their best. I tried to be honest with them in letting them know they wouldn't reach perfection.

But I was also honest in saying that I expected them to give everything they had in trying to reach perfection. That's what we worked toward. Let's see how *close* we can get. We won't reach 120 percent, or 110 percent, but how close to 100 percent of our potential can we get? That was my challenge to them: how close can we get to perfect?

When individuals are sincerely motivated to take up that challenge, the results are astonishing.

Slow and Steady Gets You Ready

When you improve a little each day, eventually big things occur. When you improve conditioning a little each day, eventually you have a big improvement in conditioning. Not tomorrow, not the next day, but eventually a big gain is made.

Don't look for the big, quick improvement. Seek the small improvement one day at a time. That's the only way it happens—and when it happens, it lasts.

Tough Toes Bring Hidden Rewards

In our first team meeting two weeks before UCLA's actual practices began, I would ask players to start toughening up their feet. Waiting until practices began would guarantee blisters.

I advised them against scrimmaging. Instead I urged them to start with plenty of sliding side to side, starting and stopping, making quick changes of direction, and sprinting short distances rather than long. This would gradually toughen up their feet. Players understood the need for this. They knew they couldn't hide blisters.

What I didn't tell them was that by getting their feet ready, they would also get their lungs ready. If they did the drills I recommended, their wind would be in good shape when practices got underway. Players were less inclined to pay attention to their wind. They may have felt it was less detectable.

On the first day of practice I wanted UCLA to be able to literally hit the floor running, at full speed for two hours without getting blisters or becoming winded. When we addressed one issue, the other came as sort of a hidden reward.

The Laws of Learning

The four laws of learning are explanation, demonstration, imitation, and repetition. The goal is to create a correct habit that can be produced instinctively under great pressure.

To make sure this goal was achieved, I created eight laws of learning; namely, explanation, demonstration, imitation, repetition, repetition, repetition, repetition, and repetition.

Players: Politics and Religion

I wasn't particularly concerned with what religious or political beliefs players had, but I wanted them to believe in something. "Have a religion and believe in it," I told them. "Have reasons you believe in it, but always be willing to listen to others. Then stand up for what you believe in."

Having beliefs and standing up for them go to the issue of character. What kind of man has no creed, no beliefs? What kind has beliefs but won't stand up for them? I wanted athletes who were strong on the outside and the inside.

A Leader Can Be Led

Leaders are interested in finding the best way rather than having their own way. "Because I said so" is a poor explanation for doing something. It's no reason.

Stubbornness, an insistence on having your own way, narrowmindedness, a refusal to listen, an inability to see both sides—all are antithetical to leadership. If you cling to these traits, you and whatever team you wish to lead will not progress.

The leader must make the final decision, but it should be based on his or her evaluation of the best way. The suggestions and ideas of others should play an important part in that decision. That's why a leader needs to retain an open mind.

You might remind yourself of this verse from time to time:

Stubbornness we deprecate,
Firmness we condone.
The former is my neighbor's trait,
The latter is my own.

Criticism and Praise

I took criticism from outsiders with a grain of salt. I told my players each year, "Fellows, you're going to receive criticism. Some of it will be deserved and some of it will be undeserved. Either way, deserved or undeserved, you're not going to like it.

"You're also going to receive praise on occasion. Some of it will be deserved and some of it will be undeserved. Either way, deserved or undeserved, you're going to like it.

"However, your strength as an individual depends on how you respond to both criticism and praise. If you let either one have any special effect on you, it's going to hurt us. Whether it's criticism or praise, deserved or undeserved, makes no difference. If we let it affect us, it hurts us."

It goes back to what my dad used to say. "If you get caught up in things over which you have no control, it will adversely affect those things over which you have control." You have little control over what criticism or praise outsiders send your way. Take it all with a grain of salt.

Let your opponent get all caught up in other people's opinions. But don't you do it.

Historic Loss?

The media need a story and where there isn't one they may get a little creative. The press called our loss to Houston in 1968 "historic." The game was played in the Houston Astrodome before the largest crowd ever to see a basketball game until then, 55,000, with millions more watching at home on television. The basketball court itself was set out in the middle of the Astrodome with the closest fans over fifty feet away.

Elvin Hayes, known as "the Big E," was Houston's star. Of course, the press built up the match-up he was going to have with Lew Alcindor, or "the Big A," as they suddenly started referring to him. It became a spectacle.

What was played down in all the hoopla was the fact that Kareem had missed two-and-a-half games with an eye injury, hadn't practiced for over a week, and had been confined to a dark room for several days. He had what doctors at the Jules Stein Eye Institute called double vertical vision. Kareem played hard but statistically had his worst game ever.

But, to show you how a story can be invented where there isn't much of one, the media stressed the idea of this great battle between Elvin Hayes and Kareem. It would have been a great match-up, too, except for one thing. Elvin Hayes didn't guard Kareem and Kareem didn't guard Mr. Hayes. Somehow that got lost in the effort to create drama and make this a historic game.

Later that year, we defeated Houston in the semifinals of the NCAA Championships at the Los Angeles Sports Arena, 101–69. Again they didn't guard one another, but nevertheless, Kareem had 19 points and 18 rebounds. Elvin Hayes had 10 points and five rebounds.

For whatever reasons, "historic" was never used in media descriptions before, during, or after that game. I guess Houston and UCLA had used it up earlier in the year at the Astrodome.

It was another example of why I cautioned players against believing what others said or wrote about them. Fiction often overrules fact.

Basketball in the Year 2000

Here are a few thoughts on what I'd like to see considered regarding the rules of the game of basketball.

Back in the 1940s Phog Allen, the coach at Kansas, advocated a 12-foot-high basket because he said the time would come when players would be much taller and the hoop would be too low. Phog was right. The time has come to try his idea.

I would like to see the rules committee raise the basket to at least 11 feet and see how it works. Try it selectively and then judge. Dr. James Naismith, the man who invented basketball, did not anticipate players who could stuff the ball without even jumping. How high would he put the rim if he were around today?

The three-point rule is good, although it didn't serve the purpose the rules committee thought it would serve: unclogging the middle. However, 19 feet 9 inches is too close for the three-point shot. I'd like to see them move it back farther.

Abolish the dunk, or have it count as only one point. After all, if the defense is not permitted to put a hand over the basket to block a shot, why should the offense be permitted to stick his hand *in* the basket to make a shot? If it's worth three points to make a basket from 19 feet 9 inches, how can it be worth the same from no distance at all, when your hand actually goes into the basket?

Also, add another three-point play when a team runs a screen and roll, give and go, then cuts in and makes a nice basket. That requires skill from several players at the same time. Make it worth three points. (I wouldn't really want that last suggestion to be used. I am merely emphasizing the importance I place on teamwork.)

I like teamwork. The pros don't interest me generally because of all the fancy stuff and the reduced role of real teamwork generally. The players' individual ability is truly amazing, but it has brought about too much one-on-one and less teamwork.

The colleges? That's a different story, but are we seeing them also move away from placing a premium on teamwork? I believe basketball is a team sport and should remain so.

Dealing with Big-Headedness

If I saw a player getting a little too big for his britches, too self-important, especially if he was a so-called star, I would say to some of the other players in a stern voice loud enough for the star to overhear, "You fellows are as important to the success of this team as anybody. Everyone has to fill their role for this team to reach its potential. Your role is just as important as mine. My role is just as important as anybody else's.

"Everyone on this team is equally important to the team. Nobody is bigger than the team. Nobody! Remember that."

So without directly embarrassing the arrogant player, I let him know I valued all players and the various roles they played for the good of the team.

If the message didn't get through, I would then have a conversation with the individual privately in my office and would be more direct.

I have found, however, that often people do not even realize they are acquiring this sense of inflated importance. Others see it, but they may not. So I wanted to first give the player an opportunity to make the adjustment without embarrassing him.

Of course, if the message still didn't get across, there was always the bench. What a friend the bench can be.

> Talent is God-given: be humble.
> Fame is man-given: be thankful.
> Conceit is self-given: be careful.

A Coach's Highest Compliment

One of the finest things a player could say about me after he left the team was that I cared every bit as much about him as an individual as I cared about him as an athlete.

It was important to me because I really did care about them. I often told the players that, next to my own flesh and blood, they were the closest to me. They were my extended family and I got wrapped up in them, their lives. Their problems. There was a great deal of love involved in my coaching. That's what a team should be to a coach.

Keep Priorities Straight

I stressed three important things to athletes before they joined our team and while they were students at UCLA.

I told them they were coming to UCLA to get an education, a degree. That, I stressed, should always be first and foremost in their minds. Their education would serve them well throughout their lives. Their physical skills would serve them only briefly.

"Second on the priority list," I told them, "is basketball. This is paying for your education, but it will be meaningful for only a short period of your life now and perhaps after graduation, except for a very few."

Third on the list of priorities was their social activities. I wanted them to be very clear that social activities were third.

I told them, "If you let social activities take precedence over your academic activities, then you will soon lose your basketball activities. If you lose your basketball activities and you lose your academic activities, then you will have no social activities here because you will no longer be a student at UCLA."

I'm very proud of the fact that almost all of my players—well over 90 percent—earned their diplomas and graduated.

They kept their priorities straight.

Walton's Whiskers

There was a rule against facial hair for players on UCLA basketball teams. One day Bill Walton came to practice after a ten-day break wearing a beard. I asked him, "Bill, have you forgotten something?"

He replied, "Coach, if you mean the beard, I think I should be allowed to wear it. It's my right."

I asked, "Do you believe in that strongly?" He answered, "Yes I do, coach. Very much."

I looked at him and said politely, "Bill, I have a great respect for individuals who stand up for those things in which they believe. I really do. And the team is going to miss you."

Bill went to the locker room and shaved the beard off before practice began. There were no hard feelings. I wasn't angry and he wasn't mad. He understood the choice was between his own desires and the good of the team, and Bill was a team player.

I think if I had given in to him I would have lost control not only of Bill but of his teammates.

Why Did Players Listen to My Old-Fashioned Message?

Simple. They wanted to play. Obviously they saw that others had gone on to successful careers in many areas after attending UCLA, so that attracted them. Our beautiful campus and fine weather were further attractions.

But basically it got down to one thing: they wanted to play. If they listened, they played.

A Key to Learning

People learn more effectively if information is given in bite-size amounts rather than everything all at once.

There was a time when I gave all my players a rather extensive, bulky blue handbook of detailed information relating to everything we were going to do as a team. Later I decided that too many of them really did not study and learn it. There was a tremendous amount of information, and perhaps it was just overwhelming. I decided to change my approach.

Instead, I began passing out information a little at a time. I found this method was productive, but it also required that I use good judgment in the frequency, amount, and type of information I distributed.

Instead of a great big heavy book of information, I gave the players individual handouts pertaining to various topics at what I considered to be appropriate times. When I broke the big subject of basketball down into small bits of information, players were much better able to learn what they needed to learn. They were not overwhelmed by the total body of knowledge.

The bite-size subjects of the handouts included goals, new rules, training suggestions, practice responsibilities, player essentials, attitude and conduct, normal expectations, academic responsibilities, criticism, game competition, shooting, push pass (both one- and two-handed), overhead pass, causes of fumbling, receiving, flip or hand-off, rebounding, tipping, stops and turns, pivoting, dribbling (high-speed and crossover), inside turn, and much, much more.

You can see why it would be less effective to put this all in a thick notebook, hand it to a player, and expect him to fully comprehend it. Breaking it down into small, easily consumed parts insured it would be read, learned, and used most efficiently and effectively.

I suspect this is true any time a leader, teacher, or coach is attempting to convey lots of information.

Negotiating and Giving Speeches

I frequently give talks around the country about my ideas and philosophy of coaching and about life. Many times my audiences are youngsters at coaching clinics.

However, when companies ask me to make a personal appearance, they ask what my fee is. I reply, "What is your offer?"

I also tell them I am not inclined to dicker. "Tell me what you wish to pay and if I say yes that's final, and if I say no that's final. And if I say no, please don't say, 'Well, we can pay you more.'"

It saves a lot of time and talk.

I've given hundreds of talks over the years. One thing I've learned is that the most popular speaker is often the person who follows "Thank you for that nice introduction" by saying soon afterward, "So in conclusion. . . ."

On Race

Dad helped set my thinking in place on the issue of race. He told me and my brothers many times, "You're just as good as anyone, but you're no better than anybody." Because of him I'm better than I might have been on many matters, even though I fall short of what I could and should be.

One of our players said to a reporter once, "Coach Wooden doesn't see race. He's just looking for players who will play together." I'd have to say that gave me about as good a feeling as I could have.

My dad was a very wise man.

Learning from Kareem

We learn from one another. When Lewis Alcindor came to UCLA (before he took the name Kareem Abdul-Jabbar), I had never dealt with anyone like him before in terms of size, his background, and other things.

I had no understanding of how tough it was for him at times. I learned more from Kareem about man's inhumanity to man than I ever learned anywhere else.

The insensitive remarks he endured that I would occasionally hear were terrible. I had never imagined that people could feel or talk like that.

He would sign autographs and more autographs and more autographs for kids outside our bus until I told him it was time to leave. Then right in front of him an adult would say, "Hey, look at that so-and-so, too much of a big shot to sign autographs." They knew I was responsible for his leaving, but they blamed him. I never saw that happen to other players.

One person said right in front of us as she looked at him, "Look at that big black freak! Have you ever seen anything like that in all your life?" Kareem was criticized in unbelievable ways. And through it all he conducted himself like a gentleman.

I tried to let him know by my actions that I disapproved of those who made unkind remarks. I let him know how wrong I felt they were.

I also told him once, "Lewis, you astonish people at times, and when people are astonished they sometimes say things they don't really mean. Furthermore, even if they meant it, please don't think all people are like that. Most people are basically good."

I learned so much from Kareem.

Athletes as Heroes

Athletes should be good role models, but not heroes. A role model is someone that those who love you would want you to be like. A hero is just someone the general public holds up to acclaim. They are often different people.

Be Careful Who You Follow

The story goes that a fellow was walking past a cemetery when he noticed a tombstone with the following inscription:

As you are now, so once was I.
As I am now, you are sure to be.
So may I say, as now I lie,
Prepare yourself, to follow me.

The gentleman took out a piece of chalk and wrote underneath the inscription:

To follow you I'm not content,
Until I know which way you went.

Choose your role models, your leaders, your teachers and coaches, with care.

Seven National Championships in a Row

If anyone had said in 1967 that some college basketball team was going to win seven consecutive national championships, he would have been locked up. But it did happen while I was coaching at UCLA. And it's just as likely to happen somewhere again—maybe even more than seven. And when it happens again I believe it will be tremendous!

Of course, there are some coaches out there I wouldn't want to break our record. But there are others out there I'd be real happy for. I'm keeping both lists to myself.

Records are made to be broken. They're not yours to keep but rather to enjoy a little while you have them.

The Pressure to Set Records

There was pressure as we approached tying or setting various records, but it was always the pressure I put on myself to get our team ready to play an opponent. That was the pressure, not an obsesssion with winning.

The real pressure during the week was put on me *by* me to make absolutely sure I did everything I could do to make sure our team was prepared properly.

I liked to think that by game time my work was virtually done, that I could almost go up into the stands and watch the game without saying a word because my team was so well prepared. I wouldn't literally go into the stands, of course, but I knew that if I did watch a team of mine from up there, I would be able to tell by their effort and performance whether *I* had done my job in preparing them during the previous week.

I was so comfortable before most games that I could take a nap if I wanted to.

Thus, when UCLA was establishing various records, I believe the rest of my family got more excited about it than I did. Though I was pleased with the titles and championships, I mainly derived satisfaction from the preparation and knowing that I had done everything I could do to get the team ready. That is what pleased me most, regardless of what anybody else thought, be they the alumni, the public, or the media. As Pearl Mesta said, "Those that matter don't mind and those that mind don't matter." The praise or criticism you receive elsewhere doesn't matter. Those who know you, who really know you, that's what matters. Those who don't know you? Doesn't matter.

Reacting to the Championships

I was very happy when we won our first championship on March 21, 1964. Following the meeting with the press, Nellie and I went out for a nice dinner with the assistant coaches and their wives. The following day Nellie and I went to Easter Sunday services in Kansas City, where the tournament's Final Four was played.

It pleased me when we won our second championship the following year because at that time only a few other coaches had won two in a row.

When we won our third championship in 1967, did it have any significance? Yes, because only one other coach, Adolph Rupp, had won more than two.

Then the next year we won a fourth championship and that was nice because there were only two coaches who had ever won four of them: Mr. Rupp and me.

In 1969 we won our fifth championship, more than anyone else had ever won. It was nice, but it was not a goal.

Then we won a sixth, but we already had all the records. And then we won a seventh, and an eighth, and a ninth.

After losing to North Carolina State in the finals in 1974 we won the national championship again in 1975, bringing the total to ten.

It was pleasing, all of it, but not a goal. My players will tell you I never said to them, "Here's our goal: a championship! If you don't do it, you haven't succeeded." They understood very well what I considered success. They understood the difference between the journey and the inn.

Knowing When to Leave

As I walked across the court of the San Diego Sports Arena after the final buzzer on March 29, 1975, many things went through my mind. I was pleased we had just won our semifinal game against Louisville and would advance to the finals the following Monday night. I recalled that it was in the semis just the previous year that North Carolina State had ended our record of seven consecutive national championships.

Now we had just outscored Louisville, which was coached by my dear friend and former assistant coach, Denny Crum, 75–74. It had been a terrific game of two teams with similar styles performing well. Even though I really hated to see him lose, I didn't want him to win that particular game. We met briefly and told each other what a great ball game it had been—and it really was.

However, as I headed across the court through the thousands of screaming well-wishers and fans, I found myself for the first time ever after a game not wanting to go in and face the hundreds of lights and mikes and reporters asking the same questions over and over. I could predict what they would ask. Suddenly I dreaded the thought of doing it again. I had never experienced that feeling before.

While I was walking to the dressing room, I thought, "If this is bothering me now, after a beautiful game like this, well, it's time to get out." I just knew it at that instant.

If I had gone to the media room first, perhaps I wouldn't have announced it then. But instead I turned and headed into the locker room where all of our young-sters were. Obviously, there was a lot of excitement and noise because of the outcome of the game, but I slowly quieted things down until they all had gathered around me. Then as the players, assistant coaches, trainer, and managers listened I told them the following. "I'm so proud of you. This was a great game. I don't know what's going to happen Monday night in the championship game against Kentucky, although I think we'll be all right.

"But I want you fellows to know now that regardless of how things turn out, I've never had a team of whom I've been more proud than you young men. And that's important to me because you are the last team I will ever coach." Then there was silence. For a long time.

Nobody knew I was going to say it. My assistants didn't know. My trainer didn't know. Nellie didn't know. I didn't know it myself until just before I said it. But I knew it was time.

Later there was speculation that I had announced my retirement at that particular time to get my team charged up for the championship game. It wasn't true. I knew as I walked off the court that night that it was time for me to leave the game I loved so much. I knew it so I said it.

It was time to get on with other things.

PART IV

PUTTING IT ALL TOGETHER: MY PYRAMID OF SUCCESS

There is a choice you have to make, in everything you do. And you must always keep in mind the choice you make, makes you.

—ANONYMOUS

The Genesis

UCLA won ten national championships while I was the basketball coach, and Mr. Lawrence Shidler played a role in all of them. How big a role did he play? Let me tell you a story and then you can decide for yourself.

Mr. Shidler was a math teacher back at Martinsville High School in Indiana when I was a sophomore. Occasionally he discussed topics other than mathematics. One day in March he instructed the class to write a paper defining success. Mr. Shidler wanted to get us thinking about the concept of success and whether it just meant getting rich or famous or beating somebody in a ball game.

Well, this got me thinking hard about the subject, and I continued thinking about it for a long time after I completed Mr. Shidler's homework assignment. In fact, I reflected on it for decades.

Later, when I entered the teaching and coaching profession after graduating from Purdue, the question continued to intrigue me because I found myself a little bit disillusioned with what seemed to be expected from youngsters under my supervision in classrooms.

Are You a Failure if You Do Your Best?

Parents wanted their children in my English classes at South Bend Central to receive an A or a B even though many were not capable of earning that. The parents judged an A or B as success and anything else as failure.

Keep in mind that most of us are about average, and C is an average grade. For parents to think their youngster, a child who might have only average ability in English, had *failed* with an average grade after performing to the *best* of his or her ability seemed unfair to me.

Apparently the grade of C was all right for their neighbor's child but not for their own. It brought to mind Mr. Shidler's assignment: what exactly is success (and failure)?

Did You Really Win if You Gave a Second-Rate Effort?

I didn't like these parents' way of measuring success and failure because it was unfair. I felt a child who worked very hard, tried his or her very best, and received a C grade had a higher level of personal success than a more gifted youngster who got a B but didn't put forth a full effort.

I began searching for some way that would not only make me a better teacher but give the youngsters under my supervision something to aspire to that was more productive, more fair, and more rewarding.

Recalling Dad's Words

In struggling to find an answer to the question Mr. Shidler had posed years before, I recalled what my dad had constantly tried to get across to us when we were growing up back on the farm: don't worry much about trying to be better than someone else.

Now that may seem a little strange to you. You might not comprehend its true meaning if that was all he had said. However, Dad always added the following. "Always try to be the very best that *you* can be. Learn from others, yes. But don't just try to be better than they are. You have no control over that. Instead try, and try very hard, to be the best that you can be. That you have control over. Maybe you'll be better than someone else and maybe you won't. That part of it will take care of itself."

Those were strong words. I remembered them in trying to give my students something to which they could aspire other than just a higher mark.

I also wanted something more productive and rewarding for the athletes I was coaching in football, tennis, basketball, and baseball. I didn't want points to be the final measurement of their achievement or success.

It seemed to me that it was possible to win and be outscored, or to lose even when you outscored an opponent. I thought so then and I still do.

Creating My Definition of Success

I thought about what my father had said, Mr. Shidler's writing assignment on success, and a verse I happened to read at about this time:

> At God's footstool to confess,
> A poor soul knelt and bowed his head.
> "I failed." he cried. The Master said,
> "Thou didst thy best, that is success."

Keeping all these in mind, I finally coined my definition in 1934.

> Success is peace of mind that is the direct result of self-satisfaction in knowing you did your best to become the best that you are capable of becoming.

Furthermore, only one person can ultimately judge the level of your success—you. Think about that for a moment.

I believe that is what true success is. Anything stemming from *that* success is simply a by-product, whether it be the score, the trophy, a national championship, fame, or fortune. They are all by-products of success rather than success itself, indicators that you perhaps succeeded in the more important contest.

That real contest, of course, is striving to reach *your* personal best, and that is totally under your control. When you achieve that, you have achieved success. Period! You are a winner and only you fully know if you won.

You Are Different; I Am Different

Obviously, the Good Lord in his infinite wisdom didn't make everyone alike or put everyone in the same environment. Some of us are shorter or taller, quicker or slower, smarter or otherwise. Situations vary. Some people have more opportunities, some less.

We are not the same in all these things, but we are all the same in *having the opportunity to make the most of what we have, whatever our situation.*

The ultimate challenge for you is to make the attempt to improve fully and be your best in the existing conditions.

I wanted to get this idea across to the youngsters I was teaching. I wanted them to know that making the very most of what *you* have is success and that it is something you control. I wanted the athletes I was coaching to understand this as well.

The Hard Part Is Still Ahead

Having defined what I believe success truly is, I recognized there was an even greater task before me: to fully understand and then describe what was necessary to achieve this success, both individually and as a member of a basketball team or any other team in life. Without this second part, it would be like going on a trip in your car if you knew where you wanted to go but didn't know how to get there. You might correctly be described as going nowhere.

What does it take to achieve success, to get where I knew I wanted to go? I began a long search for the answers.

Ten National Championships

What I eventually discerned led to something that got a lot of attention—those records established by UCLA basketball teams: ten national championships, seven of them in consecutive years, the undefeated seasons, and the 88-game winning streak. But, more than that, it provided me with a guide, a standard of preparation and performance, that brought me the greatest peace of mind in all areas of my life.

I believe it provided the same for many of those whom I taught.

Finding the Answers: The Pyramid

One day I saw an illustration that helped lead me to the answers I was looking for. It was called the ladder of achievement.

The author had taken a ladder with five rungs and had given each rung of that ladder a name describing something he thought was necessary to get to the top of the ladder.

Naturally I could not use the ladder idea, and I had a completely different notion of what the top consisted of. But it gave me the idea for what became the Pyramid of Success.

I decided that the individual blocks of the Pyramid would consist of those personal qualities necessary for achieving success according to my definitions: peace of mind that is the direct result of self-satisfaction in knowing you did your best to become the best you are capable of becoming.

Building the Pyramid Took Years

Each block in the Pyramid was selected with meticulous care and consideration over many years and after a variety of experiences in my life. Some of the blocks selected

Success

Success is peace of mind that is a direct result of self-satisfaction in knowing you did your best to become the best you are capable of becoming.

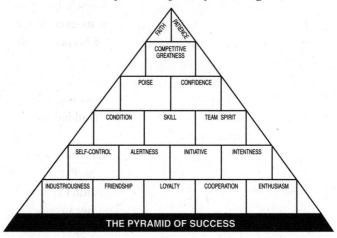

in the early years were discarded when I concluded they were less than essential. Other blocks were put in different positions within the structure as I learned more with time.

The position of each block and the specific order of the tiers of blocks in the Pyramid have great importance, starting with the foundation and cornerstones and building up to the apex: your own personal success.

Building a Solid Foundation for Success

In 1934 I chose two blocks as the cornerstones of my Pyramid of Success without any clear knowledge of how many blocks it would eventually have or its eventual size. That would come only after hundreds of hours of reflection over a period of fourteen years.

I did know that at the top of the Pyramid, at the apex, was success as defined by many of the teachings Dad had given us back on the farm. To those I added my own ideas gained from experience.

So in 1934 I began by putting in place two huge and powerful blocks as the cornerstones of the Pyramid, two fundamental personal qualities that I wouldn't change if I had to do it over again today in 1997, because without them you *will not succeed*. These are the biggest and most essential blocks in the Pyramid: industriousness and enthusiasm. Let me tell you a little about both of them.

The First Cornerstone: Industriousness

Industriousness? I mean very simply that you have to work and work *hard*. There is no substitute for work. Worthwhile things come only from work.

I challenge you to show me one single solitary individual who achieved his or her own personal greatness without lots of hard work.

Michael Jordan? More important than his physical ability is the way he has worked hard to improve any weaknesses he had. Jack Nicklaus? Mr. Nicklaus is legendary for his hard work. Cal Ripken Jr.? The same. And anyone else you might care to mention who has achieved personal success and competitive greatness. Businessperson, clergy, doctor, lawyer, plumber, artist, writer, coach or player, all share a fundamental trait. They work very hard. More than that, they love the hard work.

You may suggest that Babe Ruth achieved greatness even though he broke training in every sort of way over and over again. But just imagine what he might have done if he had focused on bringing out the best that he had within him.

He may have achieved greatness in the eyes of many, but did he achieve his own personal greatness? Did he try to be the best that he could be?

Short Cuts

Hard work is essential, and only you really know if you're giving it everything you've got. People who always try to cut corners will never come close to realizing their full potential.

Grantland Rice understood this when he wrote "How To Be a Champion."

> You wonder how they do it,
> You look to see the knack,
> You watch the foot in action,
> Or the shoulder or the back.
>
> But when you spot the answer
> Where the higher glamours lurk,
> You'll find in moving higher
> Up the laurel-covered spire,
> That most of it is practice,
> And the rest of it is work.

So I chose work as the first cornerstone in the Pyramid of Success. I call it industriousness to make very clear it involves more than merely showing up and going through the motions. Many people who tell you they worked all day weren't really working very hard at all, certainly not to the fullest extent of their abilities.

Industriousness is the most conscientious, assiduous, and inspired type of work. A willingness to, an appetite for, hard work must be present for success. Without it you have nothing to build on.

You can work without being industrious, but you can not be industrious without work.

The Other Cornerstone: Enthusiasm

On the other side of the Pyramid foundation is my second powerful cornerstone: enthusiasm. By that I mean simply that you have to like what you're doing; your *heart* must be in it. Without enthusiasm you can't work up to your fullest ability.

I have a little problem with those who complain about their jobs—coaches who tell me how hard their job is, businesspeople who whine about this or that, teachers who complain about how tough they have it working with youngsters. Gracious sakes alive! The opportunity to teach and coach and work with youngsters hard? I believe otherwise.

And I believe it's true in any profession. If you're knocking it all the time, get out! Don't whine, complain, or criticize. Just leave. Maybe you can't leave immediately, today, right now, but understand you must eventually do it.

Because if you don't enjoy your endeavors, it is almost impossible to have enthusiasm for them. And you must have enthusiasm to prepare and perform with industriousness. Enthusiasm ignites plain old work and transforms it into industriousness.

Enthusiasm brushes off on those with whom you come into contact, those you work with and for. You must have enthusiasm, especially if you're a leader or if you wish to become a leader.

Leadership Requires Enthusiasm

People in positions of leadership have many responsibilities. They have to influence those under their supervision in a positive way. They must be interested in finding the best way rather than having their own way. Leaders must make sure that those under their supervision understand that they're working *with* the leader, not *for* the leader.

But, most important, leaders must always generate enthusiasm if they wish to bring out the best in themselves and those under their supervision.

Regardless of whether you're leading as a teacher, coach, parent, or businessperson, or you're a member of a leadership team, you must have enthusiasm. Without it you cannot be industrious to the full level of your ability. With it you stimulate others to higher and higher levels of achievement.

So as the cornerstones of the Pyramid of Success I placed these two essential qualities: industriousness and enthusiasm. You must be willing to work hard, to be industrious. You must join that with enthusiasm. Separately each is powerful in its own particular way. Joined together they become a force of almost unimaginable power.

You need those qualities within yourself. And if you are a leader, you will soon instill those qualities in those under your supervision by your example.

Between the Cornerstones: The Foundation

No structure is going to be very strong and solid unless it has a sturdy foundation. The blocks in between my two cornerstones make a strong and solid foundation because they include others, and when we include others we're adding tremendous strength.

Those additional blocks of the foundation are friendship, loyalty, and cooperation. Their great importance is that they bring together and amplify the qualities at the cornerstones: industriousness and enthusiasm. The additional blocks show that it takes united effort to succeed.

Friendship

For success, either individually or for your team, there must be a level of friendship. It is a powerful force that comes from mutual esteem, respect, and devotion.

It isn't friendship when someone does something nice for you. He or she is simply being a nice person. Friendship is mutual; doing good things for each other. There's no real friendship when only one side is working at it. Both must give for there to be friendship.

Friendship takes time and understanding. Rarely will you find in working toward a common goal that others will be able to resist friendship if you offer it sincerely and openly. However, you may have to prime the pump first. Be brave enough to offer friendship.

Toward the end of the Civil War, reparations were being discussed in the White House. Abraham Lincoln was told by one of his advisors who favored punishing the South, "Mr. President, you're supposed to destroy your enemies, not make friends of them!"

Mr. Lincoln replied, "Am I not destroying an enemy when I make a friend of him?" He understood the tremendous force of friendship. Friendship includes others and adds strength to your foundation.

Loyalty

My goodness, how can you work to the best of your ability unless you have someone or something to whom you are loyal? Only then do you gain peace and an increasing ability to perform at your highest level.

Loyalty to and from those with whom you work is absolutely necessary for success. It means keeping your self-respect, knowing who and what you have allegiance to. It means giving respect to those you work with. Respect helps produce loyalty.

Great loyalty was stressed on all my teams, from Indiana State Teachers College to UCLA. Loyalty is a cohesive force that forges individuals into a team.

Loyalty is very important when things get a little tough, as they often do when the challenge is great. Loyalty is a powerful force in producing one's individual best and even more so in producing a team's best.

Cooperation

In order to reach the full potential of the group, there must be cooperation at all levels. This means working together in all ways to accomplish the common goal. And to get cooperation, you must give cooperation.

You are not the only person with good ideas. If you wish to be heard, listen. Always seek to find the best way rather than insisting on your own way.

All of this requires cooperation. It allows individuals to move forward together, to move in the same direction instead of going off in different directions.

Ten strong field horses could not pull an empty baby carriage if they worked independently of each other. Regardless of how much effort they exerted individually, the carriage wouldn't budge without their mutual cooperation.

Building on the Solid Foundation: Self-Control, Alertness, Initiative, and Intentness

No edifice is going to be better than its structural foundation, just as no individual is better than his or her mental foundation. Those five blocks—friendship, loyalty, cooperation, and the powerful cornerstones of industriousness and enthusiasm—are the strong and sturdy foundation upon which you build success.

Once this had been constructed I put in place the second tier, four blocks that build on the solid foundation: self-control, alertness, initiative, and intentness.

Self-Control

Self-control is essential for discipline and mastery of emotions, for discipline of self and discipline of those under your supervision.

You cannot function physically or mentally unless your emotions are under control. That is why I did not engage in pregame pep talks to stir emotions to a sudden peak.

I preferred to maintain a gradually increasing level of both achievement and emotions rather than trying to create artificial emotional highs. For every contrived peak you create, there is a subsequent valley. I do not like valleys. Self-control provides emotional stability and fewer valleys.

Remember, discipline of others isn't punishment. You discipline to help, to improve, to correct, to prevent, not to punish, humiliate, or retaliate.

When you punish you antagonize. You cannot get the most positive results when you antagonize. Self-control is essential to avoid antagonizing.

When you lose control of your emotions, when your self-discipline breaks down, your judgment and common sense suffer. How can you perform at your best when you are using poor judgment?

In the many years before we won a championship I overcame disappointment by not living in the past. To do better in the future you have to work on the "right now." Dwelling in the past prevents doing something in the present.

Complaining, whining, making excuses just keeps you out of the present.

That's where self-control comes in. Self-control keeps you in the present.

Strive to maintain self-control.

Alertness

Alertness is the next building block in the Pyramid. There is something going on around us at all times from which we can acquire knowledge if we are alert. Too often we get lost in our own tunnel vision and we don't see the things that are right in front of us for the taking, for the learning.

My favorite American hero is Abraham Lincoln. He had alertness. He once said that he never met a person from whom he did not learn something, although most of the time it was something *not* to do. That also is learning, and it comes from your alertness.

As you strive to reach your personal best, alertness will make the task much easier. Be observing constantly, quick to spot a weakness and correct it or use it, as the case may warrant.

Initiative

You must not be afraid to fail. Initiative is having the courage to make decisions and take action. Keep in mind that we all are going to fail at times. This you must know. None of us is perfect. But if you're afraid of failure, you will never do the things you are capable of doing.

I always cautioned my teams, "Respect your opponents, but never fear them. You have nothing to fear if you have prepared to the best of your ability."

Never fear failure. It is something to learn from. You have conquered fear when you have initiative.

Intentness

The fourth block in the second tier of the Pyramid of Success is intentness. I could say it means determination. I could say it means persistence. I could say it means tenacity or perseverance.

I will say it is the ability to resist temptation and stay the course, to concentrate on your objective with determination and resolve.

Impatience is wanting too much too soon. Intentness doesn't involve wanting something. It involves doing something.

The road to real achievement takes time, a long time, but you do not give up. You may have setbacks. You may have to start over. You may have to change your method. You may have to go around, or over, or under. You may have to back up and get another start. But you do not quit. You stay the course. To do that, you must have intentness.

Here's a little example of what I mean. In 1948 I began coaching basketball at UCLA. Each hour of practice we worked very hard. Each day we worked very hard. Each week we worked very hard. Each season we worked very hard. For fourteen years we worked very hard and didn't win a national championship. However, a national championship *was* won in the fifteenth year. Another in the sixteenth. And eight more in the following ten years.

Be persistent. Be determined. Be tenacious. Be completely determined to reach your goal. That's intentness.

If you stay intent and your ability warrants it, you will eventually reach the top of the mountain.

Three More Strong Blocks: Condition, Skill, and Team Spirit

In the third tier I put what I think is the heart of the Pyramid. It may seem to apply to athletics alone, but it doesn't. The personal characteristics in the third tier apply equally to individuals and teams anywhere.

These blocks are condition, skill, and team spirit.

Condition

You must be conditioned for whatever you're doing if you're going to do it to the best of your ability. There are different types of conditioning for different professions. A deep-sea diver has different conditioning requirements from a salesperson. A surgeon has different physical conditioning requirements from a construction worker. A CEO has different conditioning requirements from a food server.

You must add to physical conditioning mental and moral conditioning. I stressed all forms of conditioning for my teams.

Some believed my players were simply in better physical condition than the competition. They may have been, but they also had tremendous mental and emotional conditioning.

You must identify your conditioning requirements and then attain them. Without proper conditioning in all areas, you will fall short of your potential.

It is impossible to attain and maintain desirable physical condition without first achieving mental and moral condition.

Skill

At the very center of the Pyramid is skill. You have to know what you're doing and be able to do it quickly and properly.

I had players at UCLA who were great shooters. Unfortunately they couldn't get off any shots so they didn't help us. I had players who could get off plenty of shots but couldn't shoot a lick. You need both; the ability to do it quickly and *properly*.

Skill means being able to execute all of your job, not just part of it.

It's true whether you're an athlete or an attorney, a surgeon or a sales rep, or anything else. You'd better be able to execute properly and quickly. That's skill. As much as I value experience, and I value it greatly, I'd rather have a lot of skill and little experience than a lot of experience and a little skill.

Team Spirit

The last block in the third tier is team spirit. This means thinking of others. It means losing oneself in the group for the good of the group. It means being not just willing but eager to sacrifice personal interest or glory for the welfare of all.

There is a profound difference between mere willingness and eagerness. A prisoner on a chain gang may be willing to break rocks to avoid punishment. But how eager is he?

Of course, we all want to do well and receive individual praise. Yes, that's fine, if you put it to use for the good of the team, whatever your team is: sports, business, family, or community.

Team spirit means you are willing to sacrifice personal considerations for the welfare of all. That defines a team player.

Nearing the Peak: Poise and Confidence

Near the apex of the Pyramid are poise and confidence. I believe these two important blocks of the structure are the natural result of the personal qualities that we put in place below. Poise and confidence ensue from all the other blocks.

That is why the exact order of the tiers and the blocks in those tiers is so important. I don't believe poise or confidence can come about until all the other blocks are in place.

Poise

My definition of poise is very simple: being yourself. You're not acting. You're not pretending or trying to be something you're not. You are being who you are and are totally comfortable with that. Therefore, you'll function near *your* own level of competence.

You understand that the goal is to satisfy not everyone else's expectations but your own. You give your total effort to becoming the best you are capable of being.

It takes poise to accomplish this.

Confidence

You must have confidence. You must believe in yourself if you expect others to believe in you.

However, you can't have poise and confidence unless you've prepared correctly. (Remember that failing to prepare is preparing to fail.) Every block is built on the others. When all are in place, poise and confidence result. You don't force them to happen. They happen naturally from proper preparation.

Competitive Greatness

Ultimately, all fourteen building blocks in the Pyramid of Success are necessary for competitive greatness.

What is competitive greatness? It's being at your best when your best is needed. It's enjoying the challenge when things become difficult, even very difficult.

True competitors know it's exhilarating to be involved in something that's very challenging. They don't fear it. They seek it. Is it fun to do that which is ordinary, easy, simple, something anyone can do? Not at all.

Yet most of the tasks we do in our everyday lives are very simple. Anybody could do them. They will not produce the joy that comes from being involved with something that challenges your body, mind, and spirit.

Competitors love that challenge. They know it offers the chance to produce their very finest. It brings forth their competitive greatness.

The Mortar: Patience and Faith

Just above competitive greatness I have placed patience and faith, two essential qualities that are like mortar keeping the individual blocks firmly in place. Patience and faith are really present throughout the Pyramid, holding everything together.

Patience

Most of us are impatient. As we get a bit older, we think we know more and things should happen faster. But patience is a virtue in preparing for any task of significance. It takes time to create excellence. If it could be done quickly, more people would do it.

A meal you order at a drive-though window may be cheap, it may be quick, it may even be tasty. But is it a great dining experience? That takes time. Good things always take time, and that requires patience.

Competitive greatness requires patience. Excellence requires patience. Most of all, success requires patience.

Faith

Of course, I believe we must also have faith that things will work out as they should. Please keep in mind that I'm not saying things will necessarily work out as we want them to.

However, we must believe they will work as they *should* as long as we do what we should do. And we must let that suit us. That should be satisfactory.

The Apex: Success

The highest point of a pyramid is called the apex. In our Pyramid, it is success. Above the block of competitive greatness and above patience and faith, at the very pinnacle, representing the culmination of all the qualities working together below, those powerful blocks we put in place, is success.

True success is attained only through the satisfaction of knowing you did everything within the limits of your ability to become the very best that you are capable of being.

Success is not perfection. You can never attain perfection as I understand it. Nevertheless, it is the goal.

Success is giving 100 percent of your effort, body, mind, and soul, to the struggle. That you can attain. That is success.

As a coach, leader, and teacher you're trying to bring individuals up to their greatest level of competence, and then meet the real challenge of putting them together as a group. That can be extremely difficult. The Pyramid shows the way.

As an individual you strive to bring forth your best. The Pyramid has allowed me to accomplish that, and with it, to achieve a very precious commodity: peace of mind.

What is so important to recognize is that you are totally in control of your success—not your opponent, not the judges, critics, media, or anyone else. It's up to you. That's all you can ask for; the chance to determine your success by yourself.

The Pyramid and the Players

Over the years since completing the Pyramid of Success, I would ask players to come in a couple of weeks before practice started to review it with me, to go over what it meant and how it applied to the team and themselves. I did this particularly at UCLA at the beginning of each new season.

What's surprising is that nearly every player told me later that although they didn't understand it all while they were students, the Pyramid of Success has been very meaningful to them as adults. I'm very pleased by that.

Kareem Abdul-Jabbar told a reporter he actually thought the Pyramid was kind of corny when he first saw it (you may also think this). But by the time he graduated, it had begun to make a little more sense to him. It was only later, he said, years after he had left UCLA, that it had its greatest effect on him.

Perhaps that's as it should be, because the Pyramid of Success is about life more than about basketball.

Mr. Shidler's Question

So, as you can see, I've spent most of my lifetime pursuing the issue posed in Mr. Shidler's classroom back in Indiana: What is success? It was a question that my father had already begun to answer for me with his wisdom on our little farm.

What is success? How do you achieve it? Who has it? These questions really go to what life is all about.

I do believe this: A man or woman who strives conscientiously to become the best that he or she is capable of becoming can stand tall on Judgment Day. That person will be judged a big success regardless of whether he or she has accumulated riches, glory, or trophies.

The values, ideals, and principles of the Pyramid of Success are the qualities that I believe will allow you to stand tall, now and throughout your days.

Furthermore, I believe that all of us have within us the building blocks of success. The potential is within each of us waiting to come forth. That's what you must always keep in mind. You have success within. It's up to you to bring it out.

I've been trying to do that in my own life for over eighty years. I will continue each day to strive for that until the moment the Good Lord calls me to be with my dear Nellie again.

The Great Competitor

Beyond the winning and the goal, beyond the
    glory and the flame,
He feels the flame within his soul, born of the
    spirit of the game.
And where the barriers may wait, built up by the
    opposing Gods,
He finds a thrill in bucking fate and riding down
    the endless odds.
Where others wither in the fire or fall below some
    raw mishap,
Where others lag behind or tire and break
    beneath the handicap,
He finds a new and deeper thrill to take him on
    the uphill spin,
Because the test is greater still, and something he
    can revel in.

—*Grantland Rice*

My Favorite Maxims

Happiness begins where selfishness ends.

Earn the right to be proud and confident.

The best way to improve the team is to improve ourself.

Big things are accomplished only through the perfection of minor details.

Discipline yourself and others won't need to.

Ability may get you to the top, but it takes character to keep you there.

I will get ready and then, perhaps, my chance will come.

If I am through learning, I am through.

If you do not have the time to do it right, when will you find the time to do it over?

The smallest good deed is better than the best intention.

The man who is afraid to risk failure seldom has to face success.

Don't let yesterday take up too much of today.

Time spent getting even would be better spent trying to get ahead.

It is what you learn after you know it all that counts.

Consider the rights of others before your own feelings, and the feelings of others before your own rights.

There is nothing stronger than gentleness.

You discipline those under your supervision to correct, to help, to improve—not to punish.

Goals achieved with little effort are seldom worthwhile or lasting.

Make sure the team members know they're working with you, not for you.

Be most interested in finding the best way, not in having your own way.

What is right is more important than who is right.

You handle things. You work with people.

As long as you try your best, you are never a failure. That is, unless you blame others.

Tell the truth. That way you don't have to remember a story.

Don't let making a living prevent you from making a life.

If I were ever prosecuted for my religion, I truly hope there would be enough evidence to convict me.

Although there is no progress without change, not all change is progress.

If we magnified blessings as much as we magnify disappointments, we would all be much happier.

The best thing a father can do for his children is to love their mother.

The worst thing you can do for those you love is the things they could and should do for themselves. (Abraham Lincoln)

It is one of the most beautiful compensations of this life that no man can sincerely help another without helping himself. (Ralph Waldo Emerson)

Do not permit what you cannot do to interfere with what you can do.

Be more concerned with your character than with your reputation. Character is what you really are; reputation is merely what you are perceived to be.

Love is the greatest of all words in our language.

Much can be accomplished by teamwork when no one is concerned about who gets credit.

Never make excuses. Your friends don't need them and your foes won't believe them.

Never be disagreeable just because you disagree.

Be slow to criticize and quick to commend.

Be more concerned with what you can do for others than what others can do for you. You'll be surprised at the results.

The more concerned we become over the things we can't control, the less we will do with the things we can control.

Don't permit fear of failure to prevent effort. We are all imperfect and will fail on occasions, but fear of failure is the greatest failure of all.

Being average means you are as close to the bottom as you are to the top.

The time to make friends is before you need them.

We are many, but are we much?

Nothing can give you greater joy than doing something for another.

Material things are not gifts but apologies for gifts. The only true gift is a portion of thyself. (Ralph Waldo Emerson)

You cannot live a perfect day without doing something for another without thought of something in return.

Do not mistake activity for achievement.

You can do more good by being good than any other way.

Forget favors given; remember those received.

Make each day your masterpiece.

Make friendship a fine art.

Treat all people with dignity and respect.

Acquire peace of mind by making the effort to become the best of which you are capable.